WOOD FINISHING

WOOD FINISHING

STEP-BY-STEP TECHNIQUES

Den Hatchard

The Crowood Press

First published in 1992 by
The Crowood Press Ltd
Ramsbury, Marlborough
Wiltshire SN8 2HR

Paperback edition 1995

British Library Cataloguing in Publication Data

A catalogue record for this book is available from the British Library.

ISBN 1 85223 885 2

Dedication
This book is dedicated to my wife, Di; for the many hours of typing, my
grateful thanks. Also to my sons, Mark and Richard, and my daughter Ali,
who have had less of my time than I would have liked.

Acknowledgements
Richard Barry of Southern Marketing Ltd; W S Jenkins and Co. Ltd.
Line-drawings by Noel Trimmer.
Photographs by David Marchant.

Typest by Avonset, Midsomer Norton, Bath
Printed and bound in Great Britain by
BPC Hazell Books Ltd
A member of
The British Printing Company Ltd

CONTENTS

By its very nature, finishing comes at an awkward stage in the woodworking process – at the end. Many hours may have been spent at the bench and, now, the work is assembled and looks as you envisaged it. But what next? A story of a baby cradle being taken to a maternity hospital on a car roof-rack, with the father-to-be hoping the weather was dry enough to harden off the varnish, only to find that hundreds of flies stuck to the surface, may be an extreme example. But from my own experience, if there is a deadline on 'finishing' the job, the finish is very often not taken into consideration. With this particular example, and allowing for three coats of varnish on the fronts and backs, and tops and bottoms, the finish could take six days allowing for drying times between coats – and after that handles may also need to be fitted.

Finishing is all too often an afterthought with decisions being taken in a panic situation, yet I have often heard it said that finishing is the most important part of a project. Indeed, I have said exactly this hundreds of times myself. But to put this into context, I have said it to pupils in school and to people on courses in the workshop, when all the previous stages have been completed and they are about to embark upon the final stage; at that particular point in time, it *is* the most important part. On the other hand, when you have the rough timber on the bench and are about to begin a project, the preparation and accurate planing of the material is the most important part of the work. If that is not done accurately, then all that follows will be fraught with difficulties, and problems will arise which could have been avoided if care had been taken with the initial preparation. In order to produce first-class work, therefore, each stage of the process must be regarded as the most important part – if viewed in that way, the completed project will be of top quality, or at least made to the best of your ability.

Although the finishing takes place towards the end of a project, it should be considered at the very beginning in the design stage – at the very least, the type of finish should be decided upon. If you are making a project taken from a magazine or manual, a suitable finish will normally be recommended, but if you are designing a piece of work from scratch, the finish may affect decisions taken at the drawing board. When I am commissioned to design and make a piece of furniture, say a hall table, the customer may specify that it is to be

french polished. If they do not stipulate a finish, they will expect me to advise them on what the best finish would be. I would need to take several factors into account, such as the surface finish on the other furniture in the hall or on the doors, and their basic colour and shade. Another important point to note is the eventual position of the table: if it will be tucked away in an alcove and only used as a convenient surface for a telephone and message pad, then durability does not enter into the equation, but if it will be placed just inside the front door where it may get splashed with water, durability comes very much to the fore.

The finish should not, therefore, be an afterthought. If the table is to be french polished, then very early in the design stage I will think about the possible joints that could be used in its construction. I will try to design it so that I reduce the number of corners into which I will have to polish. In that way, the finishing will be easier and, therefore, probably better since difficulty and success are related to one another.

The aim of this book is first to discuss how you can overcome the difficulties you may experience when trying to prepare a suitable surface on which to apply the finish; and second to help you decide the most suitable choice of finish and to lead you through carefully planned stages to enable you to produce professional results. It must be stressed, however, that there is no substitute for experience and it is not a good idea to practise wood finishing on projects that have taken many hours to complete. The best way forward is to begin by making up some samplers. They will be useful to keep, will involve you in the various types of finishes and will also give you some experience in handling the materials used. I would certainly recommend that you try out a finish from start to completion if you have no experience at all. Just as you would not cut a dovetail joint for a trinket box for the first time on a piece of rosewood, nor would you practise a finish on a well-made project – use the samplers instead.

Select a suitable finish, obtain all the necessary materials beforehand and then follow the step-by-step guide to its application. A few hours spent at the bench gaining experience will save much heartache later on, and will enable you to produce really professional results which will enhance a truly beautiful material.

(1) 'Care with each stage of the work will make the next stage easier.' It is a good idea to have this motto pinned up in a prominent position in your workshop as a constant reminder of its importance. Whatever you do to your timber on the bench, remember that at some time in the future, whether it be days, weeks or months, you will have to prepare the surfaces to take whatever finish you decide will be best for that particular project.

Design

The design of a project normally affects the finishing only in so far as deciding which type of finish will be the most suitable for that project, considering where in the house or garden it is to reside, and in which order the finishing should be done. In other words, it is a mental process and not a practical one. If you are a complete beginner with no experience at all of the possibilities, then the rest of the book will help you make those decisions.

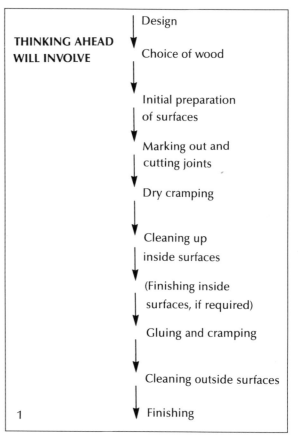

THINKING AHEAD WILL INVOLVE

Design → Choice of wood → Initial preparation of surfaces → Marking out and cutting joints → Dry cramping → Cleaning up inside surfaces → (Finishing inside surfaces, if required) → Gluing and cramping → Cleaning outside surfaces → Finishing

1

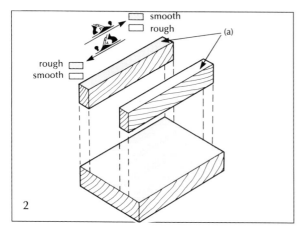

2

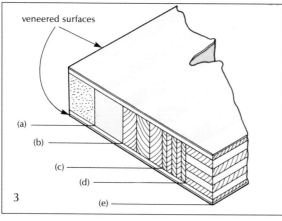

veneered surfaces

(a)
(b)
(c)
(d)
(e)

3

Choice of Wood

(2) The timber you choose for a given project can affect the time taken to finish a project quite considerably. A natural occurrence in wood which makes the cleaning of surfaces difficult is known as interlocking or alternate grain (a). The presence of this type of grain is shown by regular straight bands of light and dark stripes along the wood. The most common species in which this occurs are sapele mahogany and African walnut, although it can occur in others. Both timbers will require a lot of work with a cabinet scraper.

(3) The problem does not occur when these woods are used in veneer form and a good finish can be obtained quickly if they are purchased as 'faced' manufactured boarding. This is a good substitute for solid wood as far as the finishing is concerned, and is available in several types, the most common being chipboard (a). Other types include MDF (medium density fibreboard) (b), blockboard (c), laminboard (d) and plywood (e).

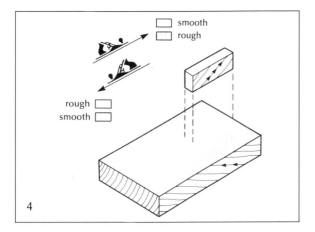

4

(5) It can sometimes be helpful to plane across the grain, holding the plane at 45 degrees. You should also be aware that if you avoid these difficult grains you miss the pleasure of seeing wood in all its diversity; the extra effort will be rewarded by a truly beautiful grain pattern. An interesting phenomenon which cross grain causes is a change in the colour of each area from dark to light, depending from which side the surface is viewed.

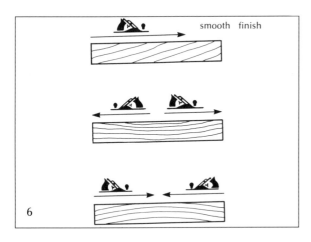

6

(6) In an ideal world, all pieces of timber would be planed in either one direction or the other to produce a good finish. In practice, though, it is rarely as simple as that. It is true to say, though, that planing *with* the grain will give a good surface whilst planing *against* the grain will produce tears (pronounced 'tares') which will then need to be removed later on.

(7) Whether you are using a hand or a machine planer, make sure the blades are sharp. Blunt blades and heavy cuts produce more tearing than sharp, finely set ones.

(4) Another type of grain which can cause difficulty is known as cross grain. Once again, the grain fibres come to the surface in different directions but instead of showing up as clearly defined stripes of light and dark, cross grain appears as light and dark patches in random areas. No matter which way the wood is planed, some areas will be rough and others smooth, and when the planing is reversed, the rough patches will become smooth and the smooth ones rough.

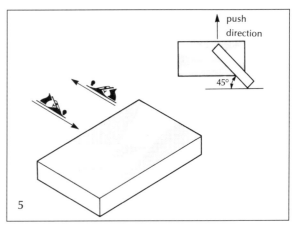

5

Initial Preparation of Surfaces

This should not be confused with cleaning up the surfaces so they are ready to take a finish. The preparation here refers to planing the wood straight, square and to size, prior to marking out joints. The way it is done can make the final cleaning up much easier. Always try to achieve the best possible finish at this stage.

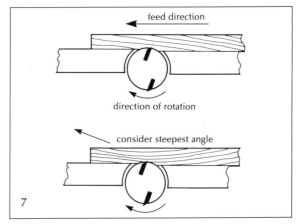

7

(8) If the grain of the wood simply waves along its length, then compare the angles at which the fibres come to the surface before deciding which way to plane. Take a close look at the ends of the piece. Quite large pieces can break off if you do plane in the wrong direction. When planing by hand, it is nearly always possible, except with the shortest pieces, to plane in each direction. One big disadvantage of planing machines is that it is only possible to plane in one direction, so when using a machine, select the best way in relation to the rotational direction of the cutters.

(9) Knots in wood always present a problem when planing because the grain runs steeply downwards before them and in a steep upwards direction after them. No matter which way you plane, the surface produced will be rough on the near side and smooth on the far side of the knot. In this case, as with other difficult grains, there is little you can do except produce the best finish possible.

(10) Hand planes have two adjustments other than that for shaving thickness which can be made. The first closes up the mouth of the plane. To make this adjustment, slacken the two bolts which hold the frog firmly in place and tighten the adjusting screw. Tighten the two fixing bolts when the correct adjustment has been made. A wide mouth will allow the shavings to be lifted in advance of the cutting edge (a) and break them off, thus giving a rougher surface. By closing the mouth, the sole of the plane will hold the fibres of the wood down until the cutting edge reaches them (b).

(11) The second adjustment that can be made reduces the distance from the edge of the cap iron (a) to the cutting edge of the cutting iron (b) to about 0.5mm ($\frac{1}{32}$ in) (c). When reducing the size of the mouth and moving the cap iron nearer to the edge of the cutting iron, neither should be so small as to allow the mouth to clog up. The shaving thickness must also be extremely fine if it is to pass through cleanly or much time will be spent in dismantling the plane to clear blockages. Much will depend on the keenness of the cutting edge and the type and grain of the wood. What is possible can only be discovered by trial and error.

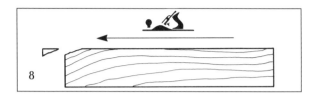

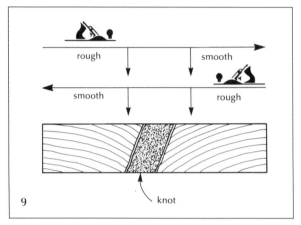

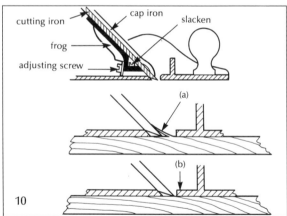

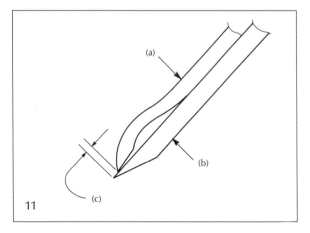

The fine adjustments that can be made to hand planes, together with the scope for planing in both directions, make them the best tool for the job in hand, which is to produce the best surface possible at the initial preparation stage. The machine planer, on the other hand, has the ability to plane the wood true and to size efficiently in terms of time and effort. If you do have a planer/thicknesser, then you have the best of both worlds.

(12) On my own work, I use the machine to trim up the wood and bring it to size, but allow at least 1mm ($\frac{1}{16}$ in) to finish with hand tools. Most tears will be less than that in depth, and by planing in both directions most of these can be removed without too much work at the bench **(13)**. This process will work only with wavy grain; the problems caused by difficult grains as described earlier will still remain. If the wood is of a very even grain, the machine can be used to bring it to size, allowing just enough to remove the ripples.

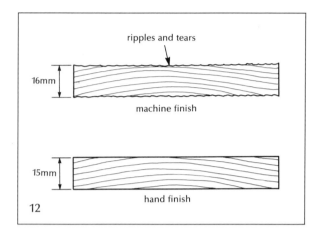

12

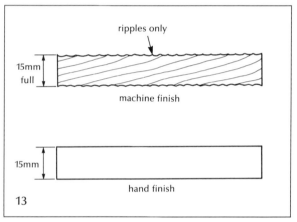

13

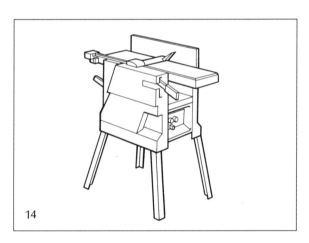

14

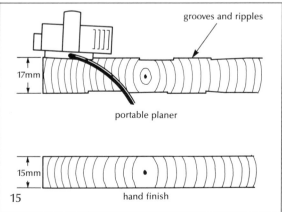

15

(14) In all considerations on planing so far, the machine to which I have referred has been a free-standing, floor-mounted planer/thicknesser.

(15) Before I leave the subject of planing, mention should be made of hand-held power planes. These can be useful when you need to reduce wood quickly to size, but they do have certain limitations. With careful use and a lot of practice they can do a reasonable job, but allowance must be made not only to remove tears and ripples by hand, but also to remove the grooves they leave, particularly when they are used on wide boards. Care is the keyword when using these tools: always use sharp cutters and take finer cuts as you near the finished thickness; and I recommend you use tipped blades.

Care When Marking Out

Still with the idea of making life easier later on, the next stage in the project will be to set out the material and mark out the joints. If you are working to traditional cabinet-making methods, you will already have selected and marked the face side and face edge on each piece of wood during the planing stages. *Do not be afraid to change your mind*. It is silly to stick rigidly to previous decisions just because the face marks are pencilled on the wood – for example, you may discover, when setting out all the pieces, that there is a better grain or colour match on other surfaces. If you do not want anyone to know you have changed your mind, then a two-second burst with a cabinet scraper will ensure that no one will be any the wiser.

With regard to pencils, it is worth noting that even these can cause difficulty later on, and can make the important stage of preparing surfaces to take a finish more difficult. Pencils are used for face marks and for numbering joints and, in some cases, for marking the joints themselves. They are graded according to the hardness or softness of the lead. A 5H or 6H is hard enough to cut into the fibres of the wood, particularly on softwoods; if you use a 2B, 3B or softer, then the blackness of the lead will be rubbed into the grain, particularly on pine and light-coloured hardwoods, and this is difficult to remove later. From my own experience, I advise you to use HB for face marks and numbers, and a 2H for joint work where required. On all woods, try to keep the wood as clean as possible.

In a purpose-built workshop with a sink and running water, keeping hands clean is not a problem – it just takes a little time and effort to walk to the sink. I can appreciate, though, that if you are working in a garage or shed some distance from the house, where washing facilities are not available, it can be a problem, both in terms of time wasted and inconvenience. A tub of 'wet-wipes' (the sort you might keep in the glove compart-ment of the car for a family day out) solve the problem. Keep them by the bench and use them regularly, but particularly after sharpening tools and handling cramps. An alternative would be a damp flannel and some washing-up liquid.

Light darkens the surface of wood. Bright sunlight speeds up the process. If you leave your wood for more than a day or so, it is best to cover it up with a thick cloth.

WHEN MARKING OUT AVOID:

- Very hard pencils – 3H, 4H, 5H, 6H
- Very soft pencils – B, 2B, 3B
- Felt-tip pens – they will penetrate deeply into the grain
- Ball-point pens – they pick up dust and spread ink into the grain
- Coloured pencils
- Rubbing out wrong marks with a rubber
- Handling wood with dirty hands, for example, after sharpening tools
- Handling oak, mahogany and chestnut with moist hands – they turn the wood blue
- Placing small objects on large surfaces and leaving them for days. The area around the object will darken leaving a light area under the object. Sunlight will speed the process up
- Placing refreshments on any part of the work

WHEN MARKING OUT DO:

- Use an HB pencil for face marks and numbers
- Use a 2H pencil for joint work
- Use a marking knife for all 'cut' lines across the grain
- Use a gauge for all 'cut' lines with the grain
- 'Spot' the wood to prevent gauge run-over

WHEN MARKING OUT DO NOT:

- Be afraid to change your mind
- Make gauge or knife lines too deep

16

If you were to leave a plank on the bench with a plane resting in the middle of it, then the area beneath the plane will remain the same colour as when you left it, but the surrounding wood will have darkened. This situation is best avoided.

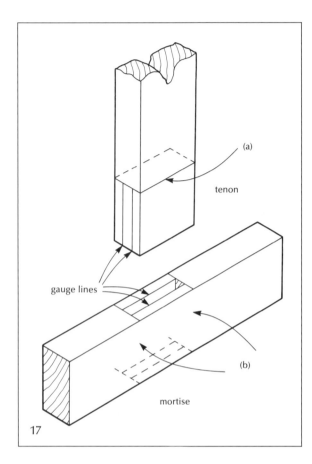

gauge lines

tenon

(a)

(b)

mortise

17

When marking out joints, it is good practice to use a marking knife for all 'cut' lines across the grain and a gauge for all 'cut' lines with the grain as these are more accurate than pencils. By 'cut' lines I mean lines that you will later cut back to with either a saw, chisel or other cutting tool. These lines present a particular hazard for later finishing – you do not want them where they are not required. An experienced craftsman will be able to anticipate where the lines are needed and where they are not, but for the less experienced this can be a problem and it is always best to mark out, and indeed cut, an unfamiliar joint on spare timber first. This gives you the chance to see if it is right, gives you bench experience, and shows you where cut lines are best left out.

(17) A good example of this is highlighted in the mortise and tenon joint. Cut lines are needed all the way round the wood (a) for the tenon, but only on the two edges for the mortise. No cut lines are required on the sides (b). This applies to most other joints.

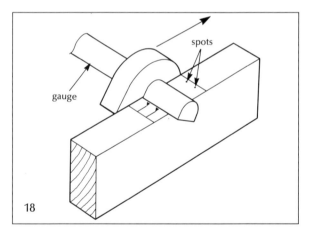

gauge

spots

18

(18) When using marking gauges and mortise gauges, it is all too easy for them to run beyond their intended stopping positions. It is always best to 'spot' the wood at the far end of the intended line just before the place where you want the gauge to stop. When the spur or point of the gauge drops into the spot, it will act as a brake and so avoid the problem of run-over.

(19) A very common fault when gauging or using a knife is to make the lines too deep. You only need a line which is deep enough for you to see and a chisel to fit into. With a gauge, the deeper the line you make, the harder it is to keep it straight because the spur will be more inclined to follow the grain; it will also be more difficult to stop it in the right place.

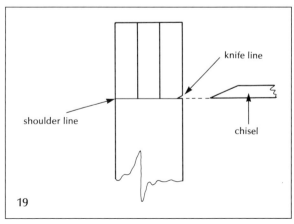

knife line

shoulder line

chisel

19

Care of Work Surfaces

(20) In an ideal world, it is best to keep a woodwork bench for woodworking. I am able to do this, but I am aware that for many people the bench in the garage doubles as a surface for stripping down the lawn-mower and repairing the children's bicycles. If this is the case, I would recommend that you look closely at your own conditions of work. Whatever the current state of your bench top, decide whether it can be brought back to a good surface or whether you need to consider relining the top with a new piece of plywood or similar board. A new layer of 6mm (¼in) thick material, for example, birch plywood (a) is sufficient as long as the old surface is in reasonable condition. Deep blemishes can be filled with car body filler (b). This could then be pinned, but preferably screwed, to the old bench top with a fairly small cost in terms of time and money. Pins should be punched below the surface and filled, and screws can either be countersunk and filled (c) or counterbored and plugged with a wood pellet (d). Having refurbished the work surface, keep a piece of hardboard of the same size to place on top, so that when the lawn-mower does need attention again, your woodworking surface can be kept in pristine condition.

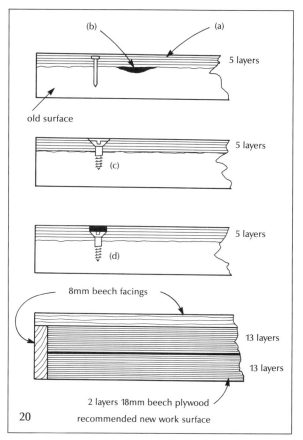

20   recommended new work surface

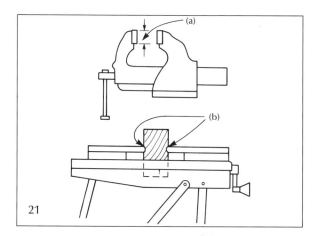

21

(22) If you must use either a metalwork vice or a Work-mate then spend a little time and make some hardwood jaws that will spread the gripping force over a larger area. A proper woodworking vice is best, and although they are expensive, they can be bought second-hand. However, even a correct vice will only be as good as the wooden jaws that must be fitted. Beech is the best wood to use, since it is a close-grained hardwood which wears well and keeps a good inside surface.

(21) Next, have a look at your vice. Metalwork vices which have small surface areas on their jaws (a) are unsuitable for holding wood, even if you have a set of fibre grips. Workmates are also best avoided for the same reason, in that they have thin gripping surfaces and bruising of the wood can occur (b).

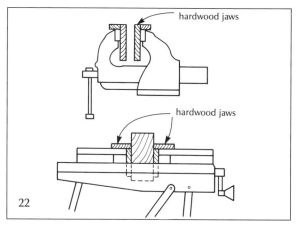

22

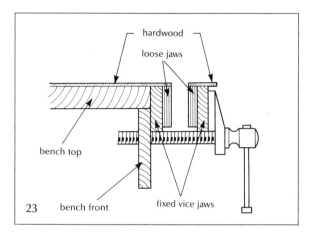

23

hardwood
loose jaws
bench top
bench front
fixed vice jaws

(24) Assuming that you have a good working surface and the jaws of your vice are satisfactory, the problems are not over yet. Much damage can be done to the surfaces of your wood if you do not keep them clean when actually doing your woodworking. Clear the bench top of sawdust and chippings before you cramp a piece of wood to the top. Beware, also, of the odd chip dropping between the vice and the work as you tighten it; keep the top of the jaws dusted off as sawdust can also leave marks when the vice is tightened (a).

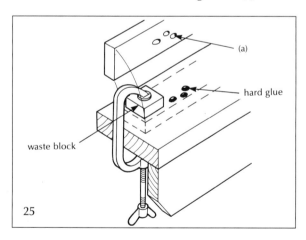

25

(a)
hard glue
waste block

(26) The best way to avoid problems is to seal your new work surface with a coat or two of varnish and then keep the top regularly waxed with ordinary furniture paste wax (sprays are not as effective). When you have finished gluing, leave all the drips to harden and then scuff them off with a piece of sharp-edged hardwood scrap. If you try to wipe off the glue before it is dry, you will spread it and the top will become very dirty and lumpy.

(23) If your workshop is a multi-purpose one, being used for other things, then even the beech jaws will be damaged if metal objects are gripped with them. It is invaluable to keep a couple of off-cuts of plywood handy which fit well, so that if, for example, you have to straighten a bicycle pedal you can slip them in place and keep a good surface on the beech ones. These can be incorporated in the hardboard protective top so that they keep this in place as well.

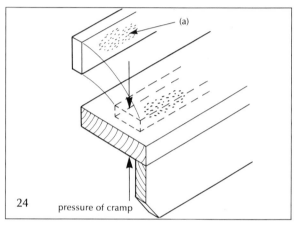

24

(a)
pressure of cramp

(25) If you glue something and forget to clear up a hardened blob of glue, this can do great damage, if you work on top of it the next day, by leaving impressions on the underside of the work (a). There are ways of dealing with this. Spreading newspaper is annoying; if you turn the work over, the paper will lift with it. The same applies to cardboard. A piece of hardboard to cover the bench is a better alternative, but this then becomes covered with blobs of glue and prevents the cramps from laying accurately, making them difficult to slide.

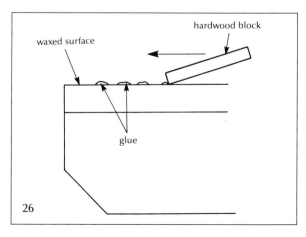

26

waxed surface
hardwood block
glue

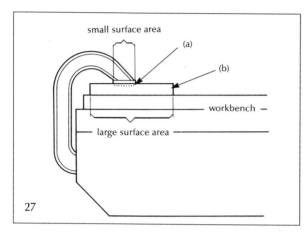

small surface area

(a)

(b)

workbench

large surface area

27

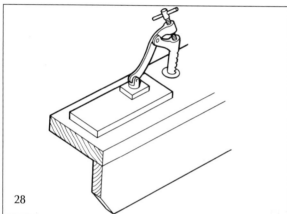

28

Care When Cutting and Fitting Joints

(27) One safety rule that *must* be remembered when cutting joints, is always to hold the work securely. We have looked at the vice, but there are other methods of holding wood which need caution if they are not to mark the surfaces. Some work will need to be held firm on the bench top, and this will necessitate the use of G-cramps, or holdfasts. These grip over a very small area and will bruise the wood (a) unless a piece of off-cut (b) is placed beneath the shoe.

(28) Do not use a small off-cut barely bigger than the shoe itself. The purpose of the off-cut is to spread the pressure of the cramp, so choose a piece of a reasonable size. Do not choose a rough piece of oak or any other hardwood if you are working with comparatively soft wood. These cause as much damage as the shoe itself. A piece of 9mm (⅜in) plywood is ideal, as is a piece of ramin, jelutong, or pine – but all must be smooth.

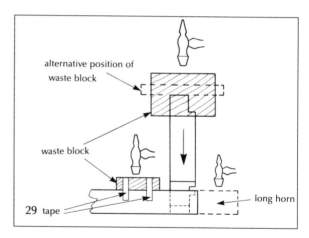

alternative position of waste block

waste block

29 tape

long horn

(29) All joints, if cut properly, should be a reasonably tight fit. In order to achieve this they will need to be tapped together and knocked apart again – maybe several times. For this job it is best to use a hammer with a piece of smooth-surfaced scrap to take the blows.

(30) A mallet is best avoided because of the size of the head and also the extension of the handle above the top of the head which can cause serious bruising or may damage a corner (a). Pay particular attention to where the scrap is placed; long horns left on the ends can be useful when knocking frames apart. Taping waste blocks in place can be helpful. Do not be over-zealous with the hammer.

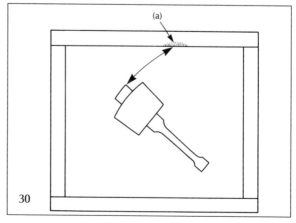

(a)

30

(31) Carcasses, such as bookcases and cabinets, generally present more of a problem than frames at this stage, mainly because the surface areas of the wood are larger and therefore more difficult to handle, but also because the possibility of leaving long horns is no longer an option on corners. The joints also have larger areas and require more fitting, which means that they have to be tapped together and knocked apart more often than framing joints. Much damage can be done to corners when boards are turned over and great care must be exercised, particularly if you are working in a confined space with a low ceiling. A heavy knock on the rafters can seriously damage a corner of a plank.

(32) Very often the construction is too high to be fitted together on the bench and so the floor must be used. It is all too easy if you are in a rush to see if a joint fits to lay the side of a bookcase on the floor, place a shelf into a joint and start to knock it in place with a heavy hammer, albeit with a piece of scrap on the top edge.

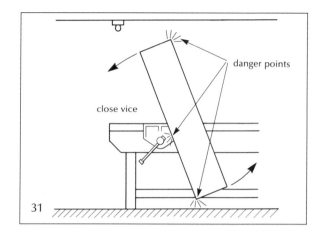

danger points

close vice

31

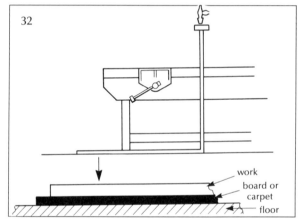

32

work
board or carpet
floor

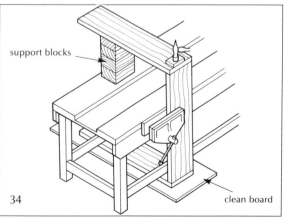

support

tape

floor

33

board

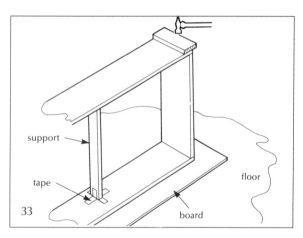

support blocks

34

clean board

(33) Stop and think of all the bruising being done on the outside surface of the job – it has been placed on all the chippings removed from the joint being fitted and the odd blob of glue from last week, not to mention the pieces of gravel which came in with you from the path. It is not really sufficient to sweep the floor, particularly if it is concrete. The best method is to lay a clean piece of plywood or hardboard on to the floor first. Alternatively, use a piece of old carpet, as I do, although it must be appreciated that some of the blows from the hammer will be absorbed by the carpet and, therefore, be less efficient.

(34) It is important to be in control of the work at all times. Fit each joint individually and take care to prevent planks from falling over and hitting the corner of the bench. Think of ways to support the wood with off-cut blocks. Damage can always be avoided with a little forethought.

Care When Dry Cramping

When all the joints have been fitted individually, the next stage is to assemble the whole job, tap in place and dry cramp it together so that the joints and overall squareness can be checked. Any twist will also be revealed at this stage, and any necessary corrections can be made. In some cases this stage will require many pieces being put together and left while another is put in place, so care taken with the fitting will certainly pay dividends. Loose-fitting joints which do not support themselves pose a real problem, especially if you are working on your own. With tight joints, you can tap each piece in place and confidently walk away to fetch the next piece. If joints are loose, you must hold them together. Sticky tape, string, or anything can be used as long as the whole lot does not suddenly collapse. If you are making a bookcase, for instance, and one shelf falls this could be similar in effect to a pack of cards, leaving damage as a result. Plan your approach carefully.

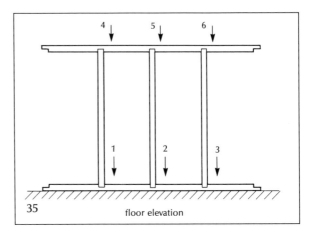

35   floor elevation

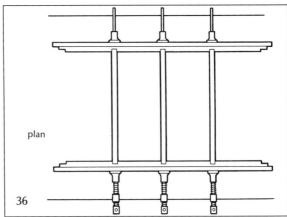

plan

36

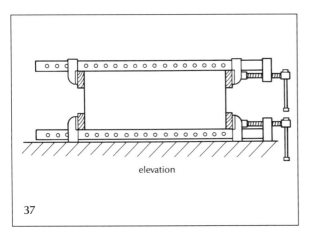

elevation

37

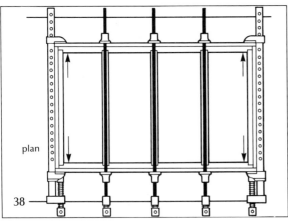

plan

38

Always ensure that waste blocks, or preferably battens, are placed between the work and the cramp heads. Battens are better as they spread the pressure more and are easier to use as they can be laid across the cramps. Blocks have to be balanced on the thin edges of the cramp bars and always seem to fall off at the crucial moment. Taping them in place can be a great help. A block falling on to the bottom of the work from any height can cause bruising and is best avoided. When you are satisfied with the fit of the joints it can be uncramped. Do not be fooled into thinking that the next stage is to glue up. Always clean up inside surfaces *before* gluing. This means the removal of all blemishes. They must be treated with the same care and thoroughness of cleaning that the rest of the work will be given. The illustration sequence shows the procedure for dry cramping: tap in place (35); lay into pre-set sash cramps resting on the bench or floor, and tighten (36); apply cramps to the top (37); spring apart to insert end boards and apply cramps (38).

Care When Gluing Up

We will assume for the purposes of this section that all inside surfaces have now been cleaned up. The best procedure for this is described in the next section (pages 24–41). Sometimes, the final finish is applied to these surfaces before gluing up, and this is also discussed later.

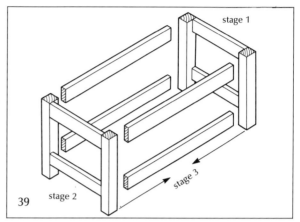

39

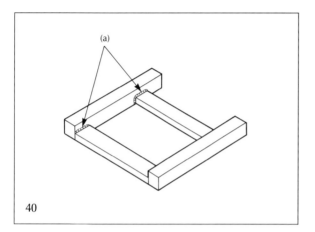

40

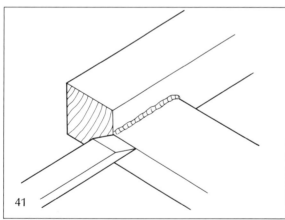

41

(39) Always glue up in easy stages. A frame such as the one shown is best done in three stages – treat each end frame separately and then cramp these together with the long rails as the final stage. This not only makes the job more manageable, but allows time to clean off surplus glue before it begins to set.

(40) As far as the later finishing is concerned, cleaning off surplus glue is as important to the work as checking the frame to ensure that it is square. If the excess glue (a) is not cleaned off immediately, it will have to be chiselled off when it is set **(41)**. It is virtually impossible to do this cleanly because the glue, when lifted with the chisel, will also lift out some of the wood fibres. If glue is simply left on the surface and nothing is done to remove it, then it will seal the surface, and even if a clear finish is used, it will always show as a light patch because the finish cannot penetrate into the wood.

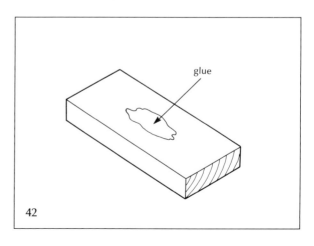

42

(42) If you want to test this for yourself, take any piece of scrap material which has a reasonable surface – just a planed one will suffice – apply a thin patch of glue somewhere in the middle and leave it to dry. Brush on a coat of clear varnish and you will see the effect. It would be much worse if you were going to stain the wood. This also emphasizes the need for cleanliness at all times when gluing up; keep a piece of rag within easy reach so that you can wipe glue off your fingers constantly.

Always allow plenty of time for final assembly. I find that all students underestimate how long it will take. It may take only ten minutes to apply the glue, assemble and cramp, assuming the equipment is set up ready, but it then has to be checked for square and twist, put right if necessary and then the surplus glue wiped away thoroughly *before* you can leave it. This is *not* a stage to be fitted in before a prior appointment; always use an open-ended slot of time. I regard it as so important that I lock the workshop door during this stage and refuse to unlock it even if someone is rattling on it.

Once the glue is applied, the setting begins. There is no time to waste as time is of the essence. Arrive at the stage where you have cramped it and made all the necessary checks as soon as possible, then tackle the problem of any excess glue. If, when you are applying glue, some of it dribbles over the edge, leave it – get the piece in the cramps first.

I am always of the belief that if a task is to be done well, you must be comfortable doing it, so when cleaning off glue, I allow myself the luxury of warm water in a clean washing-up bowl. You will also need a piece of thin rag. Thick rag does not do the job as well since you must be able to remove glue right in the corners. Another essential piece of kit is a chisel. You can keep an old one for this purpose, but it must not be chipped or it will scratch the surface of the wood. It must be honed on an oilstone and then just dulled off a little. The rag should be wetted and then wrung out, but not so much that it is too dry – it should be fairly wet but not dripping. The worst of the glue can be removed by pushing the rag into the corners with your fingers. Rinse the rag out after each wipe; if you just turn it round to a clean part, you may transfer the glue to another part of the work with the loose end of the rag.

Glue transferred to another part of the work can be difficult to see. If you take, for example, gluing together an oak chest with cascamite glue, then the colour of the glue is almost identical to the wood. This, and the fact that you are concentrating on the areas around the joints, means it is easy to miss transferred glue and it may only show up when the finishing material is applied. If this happens, the finishing material must be allowed to harden. Then, scrape the glue away with a cabinet scraper back to bare wood. Go over the area with 120 grit glass-paper and then flour paper. The lighter area produced should colour in with the rest of

---

SUMMARY OF GLUING UP

REMEMBER TO:

- Glue up in easy stages
- Clean off surplus glue immediately
- Keep your hands clean at all times
- Allow plenty of time for assembly
- Have ready a clean rag, a bowl of water, a dulled-off chisel and a small, rounded-off screwdriver
- Pre-set cramps to correct distances apart
- Check joints for excess glue after cramping
- Protect oak, chestnut and mahogany against bluing

TYPES OF GLUE:

- Scotch or animal glue – this is used hot. It gels on cooling but any excess will wash off easily with hot water.
  Resin Glues
- Polyvinyl Acetate (PVA) – a pre-mixed glue. It hardens by evaporation of water.
- Cascamite – one part powder. It hardens by chemical reaction when mixed with water.
- Aerolite – two parts powder mixed with water to make resin and liquid hardeners. The hardeners have different setting times. Place the resin on one part of the joint and the hardener on the other. Setting does not begin until the two are brought together. This can be an advantage on larger projects.

All glues set faster in warm, dry conditions. Epoxy resins and contact glues are not suitable for general cabinet work.

43

---

the work when the next coat is applied. If the work has been stained it must be re-stained first.

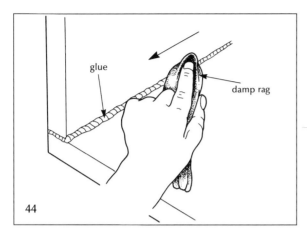

44

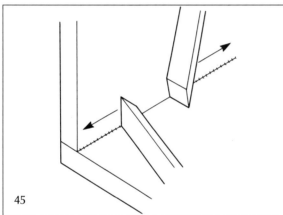

45

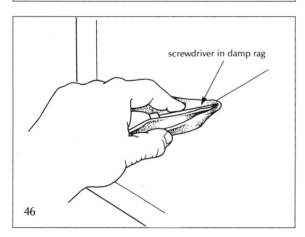

screwdriver in damp rag

46

You can prevent the card sticking to the work by smearing a thin layer of wax on the underneath surface. Newspaper will do the same job as the card but will stick to the cabinet.

(44) When you have removed most of the glue with the rag, look closely and you will see there is still more glue in the corner. To remove this use the chisel as a scraper. Place it into the corner and draw it gently across the grain of the wood **(45)**. Next, place a small, worn or slightly rounded screwdriver, or similar, into the rag and run this up and down the corner. Finish with the rag only, pushing it as far into the corner as it will go **(46)**. Do this systematically with each joint. In order to clean off the underneath, it may be necessary to turn the work over. On a large project this can be difficult, particularly if you are working in a confined area, but it is well worth the effort.

After a few minutes, go back and check each corner again. It is possible to build up tremendous pressure inside the joint when the cramps are tightened, and sometimes this pressure will push the glue out slowly, especially if you have mixed the glue a little on the thick side. Recheck particularly if you decide to tighten a cramp a little more or if you add another one.

There is one very important point to stress when using this method. Some woods, particularly oak, chestnut and mahogany, react with moisture and steel. This can cause bluing where the metal of the cramp is in contact with the wood. When using these timbers, it is a good idea to place a piece of thin card between the wood and the cramp bars **(47)**. If bluing does occur, it can penetrate quite deeply and is difficult to remove. If you are using a veneered manufactured boarding, it may well penetrate the entire thickness of the veneer.

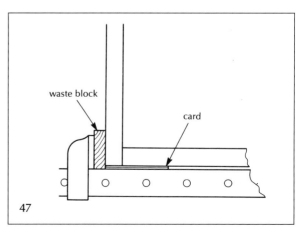

47

(48) If you are not sure whether bluing could be a problem with the wood you are using, a check can be made. Use a small off-cut. Damp the surface. Place it in a G-cramp without the protection of a waste block. Leave it for a couple of hours. Remove the cramp. If there has been a reaction a blue or purple stain will be visible (a).

(49) It is vital only to clean glue off inside surfaces, as waste glue on the outside can easily be dealt with later, when the work has been uncramped. The main reason for this is one of time. If the important parts of the work are cleaned thoroughly first, it is quite likely that the glue will have begun to set. Trying to remove it at this stage would take a lot of pressure with the damp rag, the result being that the glue would be pushed into the grain, sealing the surface – this is particularly true of end grain (a). It may do more harm than good. In any case, hardened glue will chisel or plane off easily (b). On a small piece of work where the glue is still liquid, however, then by all means clean the outsides as well.

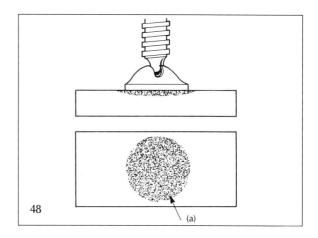

48

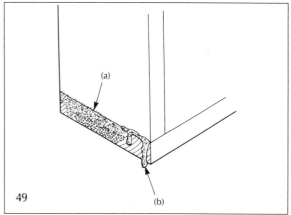

49

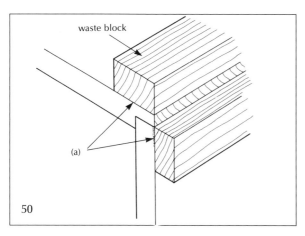

50

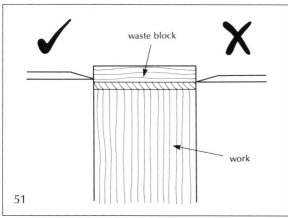

51

(50) If you have been careful when applying the glue, the problem of blocks and battens being glued to the work should not arise, but I see it happen quite often. Glue under waste blocks comes either from the joint or from fingers during assembly (a). If a tiny amount of glue has managed to squeeze between the work and block, a sharp blow on the block with a hammer will normally separate them. Hold the block, though, or it may hit another part of the work.

(51) If the hammer does not knock the block off, under no circumstances place a chisel between the work and block. The chisel will mark the surface and it is also likely that you will remove some of the cabinet with the block. Instead, place a chisel on the end of the block and split it along the grain, then plane the remaining piece off later. A way of avoiding the problem is to apply a coat of wax to the underside of the block, which will prevent it from sticking.

Smoothing Planes

Whether cleaning up inside or outside surfaces, it is at this stage that you will really appreciate the thought and care that you have put into the project since you first laid out rough planks of wood on the bench at the start. Having taken the work out of cramps, it is pleasing to realize the fact that almost half of the cleaning up has already been done, the inside surfaces having been dealt with before gluing. By following this procedure, you not only ensure a better result, but it divides the time spent on cleaning neatly into two parts, thus making the work less tedious. Follow the broad stages listed (52).

(53) The first stage is done with the smoothing plane, which was designed for the sole purpose of planing surfaces smooth prior to scraping or using abrasives. The cutting iron of a jack plane should be sharpened to a slight curve (a), this shape being more efficient for removing plenty of wood in the initial preparation of

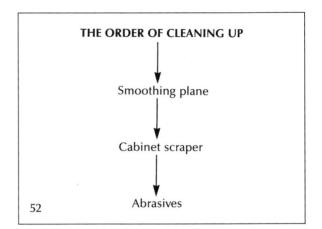

THE ORDER OF CLEANING UP

↓

Smoothing plane

↓

Cabinet scraper

↓

Abrasives

52

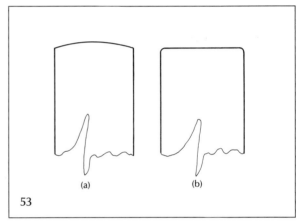

(a)   (b)

53

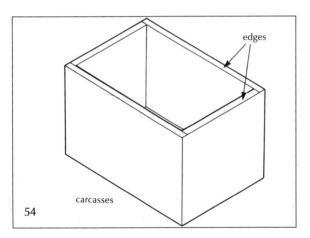

edges

carcasses

54

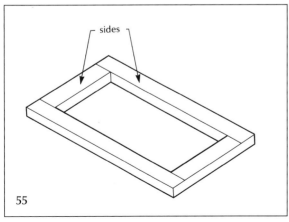

sides

55

timber for the project. The cutting iron on a smoothing plane, however, should be sharpened flat (b) with the corners rounded to prevent it digging in.

No matter how good your bench skills are, it is unlikely that all joints will have been glued together with the surfaces dead flush and level at the shoulders. This problem must be dealt with first. In practice, it necessitates planing the edges of carcasses (54) and the sides of frames (55). Whilst levelling, you will also be removing surplus glue which was not removed at the gluing stage. All glues will blunt the cutting edges of planes to some extent, PVA glues less so than those that set as hard as glass. If you have reasonable quantities to remove where the excess glue has run after being squeezed out, then it is best to use a chisel to remove the worst of it – it is easier and quicker to sharpen a chisel than a plane. Be careful not to dig the chisel into the surface, and watch carefully for glue which lifts out fibres in advance of the cutting edge. Protect your eyes when chiselling out very hard glues.

It is still extremely important to plane with the grain as much as possible. You will need to look closely at the way it runs on both pieces and try to interpret what signals it is giving you before making a decision as to the best way to proceed. Whichever way you decide, there is always a danger of breaking out an edge. Exercise great care and have the plane very finely set.

Sometimes the grain lines will tell a clear story and it is obvious which way to plane. At other times, there may appear to be no real solution and it is inevitable that at some stage you will be planing against the grain. In this case, look at the angles of the lines. One may be steeper than the other and the best finish will be obtained by planing against the one that is less steep.

Close up the mouth of the plane as much as possible and sharpen the blade before replacing it. Levelling is a difficult operation and must be done with the frame firmly cramped to the bench surface. Carcasses are

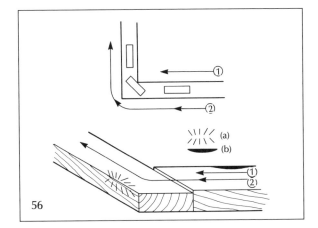

56

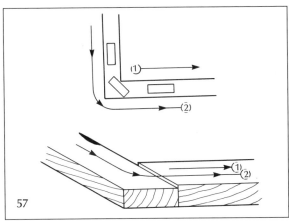

57

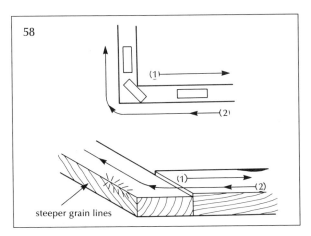

58

steeper grain lines

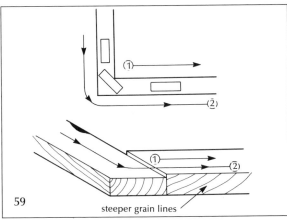

59

steeper grain lines

more difficult to hold and you will normally have to plane against stops of some kind, even working on the floor with the leg of the bench as the stop. Think of ways to hold the work still without bruising the surface which is giving support.

We are all guilty of moving the plane backwards and forwards without lifting it off the surface of the wood. However, avoid doing it now; if you continue to do so it will sooner or later result in the back of the plane hitting the inside of the carcass or frame on the return stroke. The damage caused will be difficult to disguise.

Levelling should continue until flush sides or edges are obtained and all glue and knife lines removed.

The illustration sequence (56–9) shows: the direction of planing until the work is almost level (1); the direction of the finishing strokes (2); breaking out points (a); back of plane damage points (b).

(60) Even taking extreme care at all stages, it is inevitable that some bruising of the surfaces will occur. Whilst levelling, these bruises will become apparent. Bearing in mind the fact that wood swells with moisture and that bruising is caused by a compression of the fibres, it is possible in many cases to remove bruise marks by just wetting the area with clean water (a) and leaving it to dry. A warm iron applied to the wetted area will sometimes have a better effect. The fibres will swell back to their original position (b), but it will only work if the fibres have not been broken.

(61) The next step is to plane off the horns. Short horns with good, close-fitting joints should give no problems in theory. In practice, though, if the horn is more than 1mm ($\frac{1}{16}$ in), the fibres do not tend to split but rather pull out, particularly if the wood is on the woolly side. Sometimes they will pull out below the finishing line and leave small holes in the end grain.

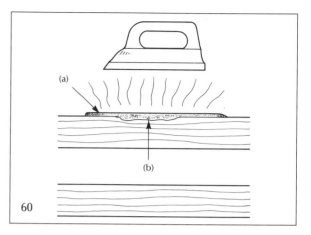

60

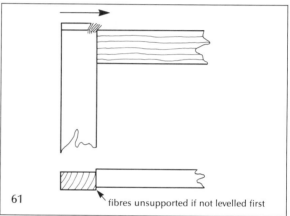

61   fibres unsupported if not levelled first

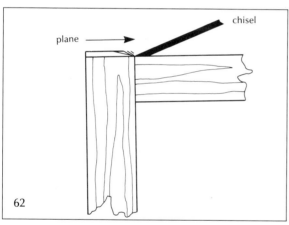

62

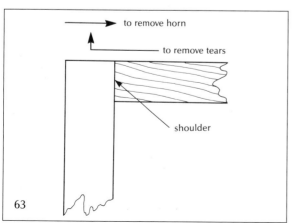

63

(62) This can be avoided by chiselling a bevel on the end of the horn and planing towards it. Keep the grinding angle of the chisel underneath and use a mallet, but take very light cuts. You will tend to knock the joint apart in some situations. This method can be used when cleaning up all joints where end grain is involved, including finger and dovetail joints. A sharp plane is needed with a little candle wax on the sole and, as in levelling, the planing should continue until all knife lines on the joint are removed.

(63) Try to obtain the best possible finish from the plane. If you are planing against the grain of the rail immediately in front of the shoulder, then some tearing may result; a couple of strokes the other way, making sure you lift the plane before it reaches the edge, will take these out. If you deal with each end of the frame in the same way, the rail in between can be planed as you would in any other planing situation – in other words, with the grain.

(64) So far, the stages in cleaning up have been clear cut – or perhaps it would be better to say 'clean cut', because if the grain has permitted the plane to cut cleanly, there is little work left to do, except glass-papering, which is the correct term for sanding. More often though, the smoothing plane will have left some tears on the surface. Sometimes these are easily seen, but on some woods they are difficult to spot – good lighting is important at all stages of finishing.

The best procedure to adopt is to use the plane first and obtain the best possible surface. Make sure it is sharp, set it finely and plane with the grain. On difficult grain close up the mouth and set the distance from the end of the cap iron to the cutting edge as small as possible (*see* page 11). Then take a piece of fine glass-paper – 120 grit is ideal. Wrap it tightly around a glass-paper block and rub until a little dust is created.

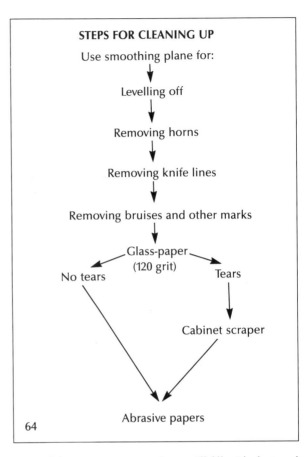

STEPS FOR CLEANING UP

Use smoothing plane for:

↓

Levelling off

↓

Removing horns

↓

Removing knife lines

↓

Removing bruises and other marks

↓

Glass-paper
(120 grit)

No tears ← → Tears

Cabinet scraper

Abrasive papers

64

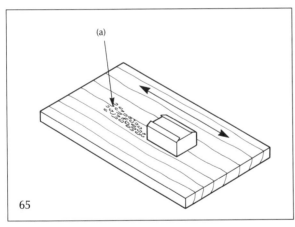

65

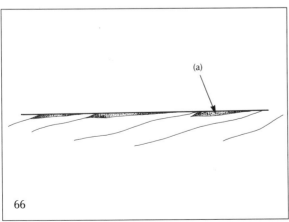

66

(65) If there are any tears, these will fill with dust and show up better as light patches (a). This applies to all woods regardless of colour. It is essential to use a fine grade of paper for this because if there are no tears, you will be using the correct grade for the final stages of cleaning up. If you use a lower grit number and there are no tears, you will make deep scratches in the wood, and to remove these you will have to work through successive grades of finer paper to arrive at the 120 grit, thus making far more work for yourself.

(66) Having pin-pointed the tears by filling them with dust (a), they have to be removed. It is possible to do this with abrasives, but even with coarse grits it will take a long time and will be very daunting if you are faced with a large piece of work. The dust produced is also unpleasant. The most efficient tool for removing tears is the cabinet scraper. They are not as widely used or as readily available as they once were, and seem to have been lost in the myth that if you cannot plug it in, then the method either will not work or it will take 'for ever'.

Cabinet Scrapers

(67) There are two types of cabinet scraper, the simplest and cheapest being a piece of cold-rolled high-carbon steel about 1.5mm (³⁄₃₂in) thick (22 gauge). There are three sizes available, the 130mm (5in) being suitable for most cabinet work. This particular scraper is also available in a shaped form for curved surfaces, and is known as a gooseneck scraper, also available in a range of sizes.

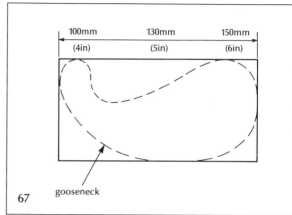

67

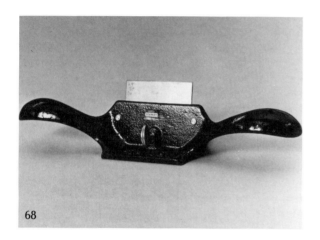

68

(69) The aim of a scraper is to produce very fine shavings. For this you need a cutting edge. The shavings are produced by fine cutting burrs on the four long corners. They are not easy to sharpen and many people are put off by not being able to achieve good results straight away. Initially, if you achieve one good cutting edge from the four, you will be doing well. Time spent perfecting the art will save many hours on future projects.

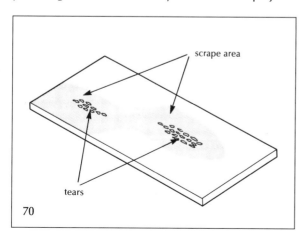

70

(68) The other form of scraper (the Stanley scraper) has a blade mounted in a frame and will do a similar job. In practice, however, you will find that it tends to be a little more coarse, although the depth of scrape is adjustable. Candle wax on the sole will make it move more smoothly.

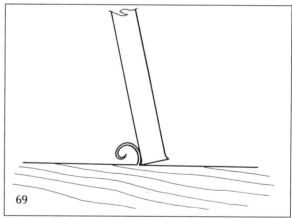

69

(70) Unless you are working with really difficult woods which have interlocking or cross grain (*see* page 10), you will never have to scrape a whole board across its entire surface. Tearing normally occurs in patches and it is these that the scraper is used to deal with, without producing a hollow in the surface. Whilst concentrating on an affected area, you will be working around it as well, thus phasing into the surface where the deepest tears are. Much will depend on how deep the tears are; you must scrape until all the light patches (shown up by the dust pushed into them) are removed.

(71) The first stage in sharpening your scraper is to file the edges square and straight (a) and (b). A smooth file is best for this, with the scraper held low in a vice. You must file along the edge or draw file (*see* diagram). Do not file across the edge. Filing will leave a rough wire edge on the corners which are then taken off with a burnisher or ticketer – a hard steel rod of about 6mm (¼in) diameter, mounted into a file handle. A screwdriver will do the job equally well, but it must be of good quality – hard steel is essential if sharp edges are to be produced, and the cheaper varieties are not suitable.

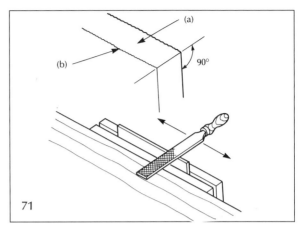

71

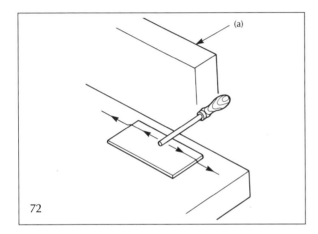

72

(73) You can, if you wish, remove all file marks on the edges (a) and take off the wire edge on an oilstone (b). It does give a slightly keener edge when the burr is formed, but it is not essential for producing a sharp burr. If you do use this method, ensure that you maintain the edge dead square.

(72) To remove the wire edge (a), lay the scraper on its side on the bench surface and run the tool backwards and forwards several times. You must keep the burnisher flat on the surface of the scraper and finish each stroke on the bench surface. Repeat the process on the rest of the corners.

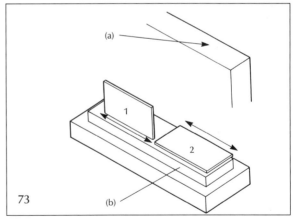

73

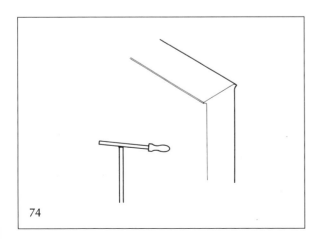

74

(74) The last stage, that of producing the cutting edge itself, is achieved by pushing the steel over to create the burr. Apply firm, steady pressure, holding the scraper in a rag with one end on the bench and the edges to be sharpened facing away from you. Use the burnisher from bottom to top, kept at a low angle of 2–3 degrees. Measure the angle with a protractor to see how small it is. Make a second stroke at about 8 degrees. Feel to see if there is a good burr – if there is not, make a third stroke, also at 8 degrees. Repeat the process on the four corners.

75 *Using a flat, smooth file to produce a straight, square edge.*

76 *Removing a wire edge with a burnisher.*

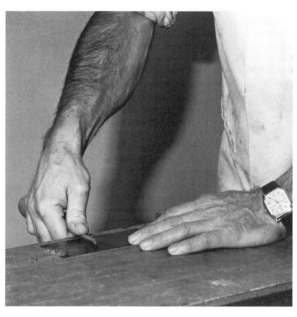

77 *Producing the burr with a burnisher. Note that the hand is protected.*

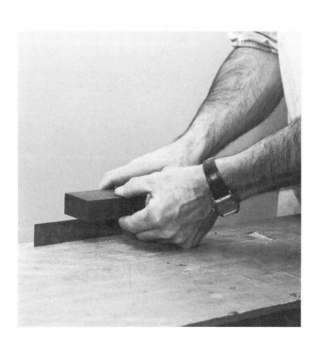

78 *Removing file marks with an oilstone.*

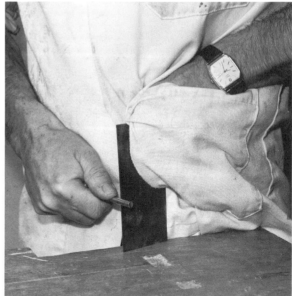

(79) A similar procedure is adopted for sharpening the Stanley scraper, but you will need to adjust the angle of the burnisher to take into account the angle at which the blade is already ground. It should still be 8–10 degrees from the grinding angle. The photograph shows the method of producing a burr on the edge of the blade of a Stanley cabinet scraper.

(80) All scrapers work by virtue of the fact that, if sharpened correctly, they will produce a very fine shaving, this being a wisp of wood that will curl off the cutting edge. If you find that only dust is produced, you must repeat the sharpening procedure. I maintain that of four edges sharpened, two will be extremely good cutting burrs, one will be not so good and the fourth will be virtually useless. It is important to sharpen all four together as they will look exactly the same and you will waste time searching for the newly sharpened ones if you only do the two corners along one edge. You can feel for a good burr by running your thumb towards the edge **(81)**.

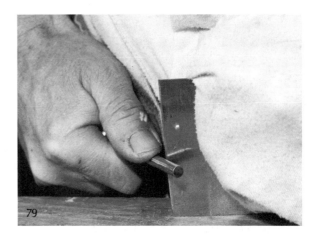

79

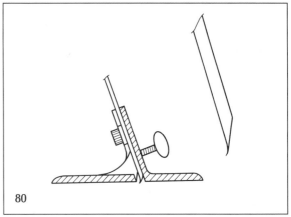

80

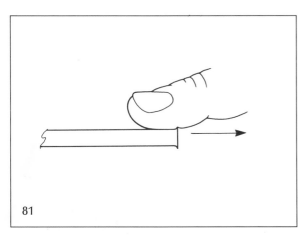

81

82

(82) There are two ways of holding the scraper. The first, and most efficient, is to stand behind it and slope it away from you. Put a bend in it with your thumbs, as shown in the photograph. As you push it away from you, adjust the angle to the surface in order to obtain the optimum cutting angle. This angle will vary depending on the angle at which you held the burnisher when producing the burr. Very often, the best results will be obtained when the scraper is held at a slight angle to the grain, but pushed in the direction of the grain, rather like the slicing action of a plane. You should still aim to use the scraper with the grain of the wood for optimum smoothness. Try to establish which way the grain is running in that particular area to be scraped. A little time spent practising the technique of using the scraper on spare timber to master it will pay handsome rewards on future projects.

(83) The second method of holding the scraper is to put the bend in with your fingers and use it from the side, as shown in the photograph. Personally, I find this method less efficient, but it does give your thumbs a rest, and by alternating both techniques it is quite a comfortable operation.

83

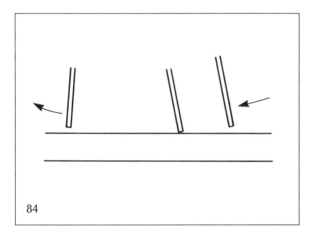

84

(84) If you are working on one area in the middle of a board, it is much better to glide the scraper into the surface and off again at the end of the stroke. If you place it on the surface and start from stationary, the start position will show as a single ripple – this is best avoided as it will be difficult to remove with abrasives.

(85) Probably the most difficult part of scraping occurs when there are tears at the end of the board or at the edges. Whether you scrape off of an end or towards it, it is important to keep more than half the blade length in contact with the surface of the wood and put weight on this part of the blade. This will prevent the problem of the tool falling over the end and rounding the corner, which should be avoided at all costs.

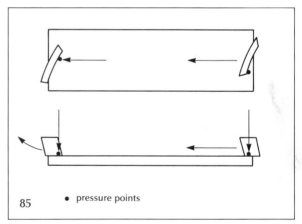

85   • pressure points

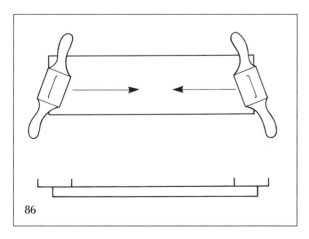

86

(86) The Stanley cabinet scraper is better for working the ends because it has a machined sole plate which can be placed flat on the surface before pushing it forwards, thus keeping the ends flat. The same applies to the edges. It is best used at an angle and set finely to avoid 'chatter marks'. In practice, if you are faced with a large board to be scraped, I would recommend that you use the fixed (Stanley) scraper simply because it has two handles to hold. Remove the deepest of tear marks with this tool. Finish with the ordinary cabinet scraper to produce a slightly better surface ready for glass-papering.

Abrasives

A good finish with a scraper will mean that you can begin using abrasives of fine grit. There are many forms of them and to the beginner, the range can be very confusing. For hand finishing, you need only paper-backed varieties – cloth-backed ones are for machines. The grades are given by a grit number; the higher the number, the finer the paper will be. The grits I keep in stock are 60, 80, 120 and the finest glass-paper, which is known as flour paper. The 60 grit is rarely used, perhaps only to remove bandsaw marks from a shaped edge or for cleaning up an awkward part of a carving. It is too coarse for normal cabinet work. The 80 grit is used a little more, perhaps to remove some tears where it would be difficult to use the scraper. As to the type of abrasive, I have found aluminium oxide to be the best. It is more expensive than glass-paper, but it is sharper and keeps its sharpness much longer. It is more open and therefore resists the tendency to clog up, and the back-

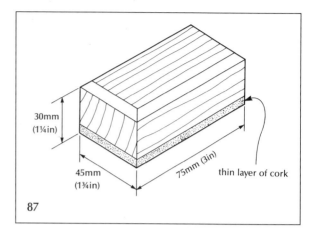

87

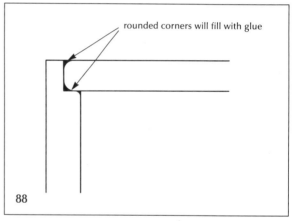

88

ing is stronger and will withstand a lot of flicking on the bench leg to keep it clean. It is readily obtainable from good decorators' merchants or by mail order from the same firms that supply finishing materials. It is available in rolls and by metre length.

(87) It is important to use a glass-paper block for all abrasives. They cut better when some pressure is exerted, and for that reason I find that the normal blocks that are sold are too large and would instead recommend the size shown in the diagram. If the paper is held with the fingers, the area exerting pressure is small and the paper will be bent and will wear out faster. The most important reason for using a block, however, is that the corners of the work must be kept sharp. This is vital when cleaning inside surfaces prior to gluing – rounded edges will fill with glue and will show up badly on the finished work (88). The paper must be folded and held round the block very tightly (89) – loose paper will also cause rounded edges (90).

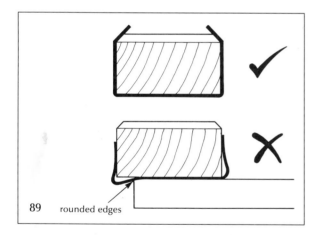

89   rounded edges

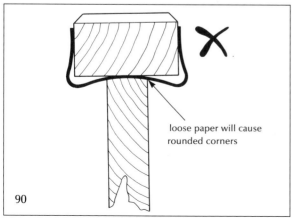

loose paper will cause rounded corners

90

(91) After scraping, I would advise that you begin with 120-grit aluminium oxide. If you compare this with 120 glass-paper, you will see that while they are of the same grit number they feel different, the aluminium oxide being sharper and therefore more efficient at removing wood. If you have done a good job with the scraper, then all that is needed is a thorough but fairly quick rub over the surface. Watch for any tears filling with dust that you may have previously missed and, if necessary, give these an extra scrape. Proceed to 120 glass-paper and go over the surface again. The object now is to reduce the depth of the scratches made by each previous grade of paper. Complete the process with flour paper. In my own experience it is not necessary to use finer paper than this, although the silicon carbide papers, known as 'wet and dry' paper, will produce a much smoother finish. It is possible almost to polish the surface with these papers before you apply any finish at all, but for most cabinet work flour paper is sufficient.

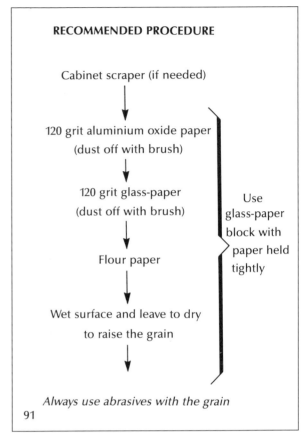

RECOMMENDED PROCEDURE

Cabinet scraper (if needed)

↓

120 grit aluminium oxide paper
(dust off with brush)

↓

120 grit glass-paper
(dust off with brush)

↓

Flour paper

↓

Wet surface and leave to dry
to raise the grain

↓

Use glass-paper block with paper held tightly

Always use abrasives with the grain

91

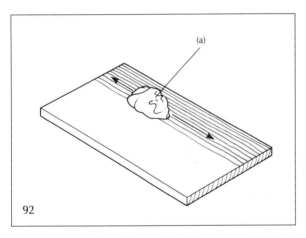

92

(92) Moisture raises the grain on wood and you must bear in mind that most finishes are themselves wet. The grain will be raised only once and it is best done at this stage. Use a damp cloth and go over the surface with the grain. The cloth should not be running with water, but fairly wet. Leave the wood to dry – this is best done in its own good time, but a hairdrier is useful for the odd part which refuses to dry off.

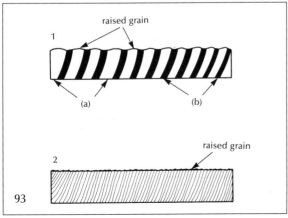

raised grain

1

(a)   (b)

raised grain

2

93

(93) You will find that what was a beautifully smooth surface is now rough again, but a second burst with the flour paper will very quickly restore it to the state it was in before. Some woods will raise the grain more than others; softwoods (1) generally raise more than hardwoods (2). The light-coloured spring and summer growth lines (a) raise more than the darker autumn and winter growth lines (b) which are more resinous and absorb less moisture. Hardwoods are more uniform and will appear generally rougher rather than ribbed.

The most common question pupils ask me when I am teaching wood finishing is: 'How do I know when the surface has been cleaned up enough?' The simple answer is 'experience', but a few pointers will help. First, do each stage thoroughly. For example, if there are tears left after scraping, none of the abrasives will take them out efficiently.

The most obvious thing to look for apart from tears are scratches. If there are scratches left from aluminium oxide paper, flour paper will not remove them. If any scratches should appear when working with flour paper, return immediately to 120 glass-paper on that area until they disappear before continuing with flour paper.

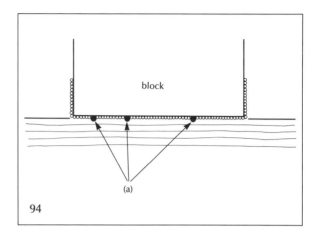

94

(94) Before moving to a finer paper, it is best to dust off the surface with a fine, clean brush – keep a special dusting-off brush for the purpose. I use a 100mm (4in) paintbrush with the steel ferrule padded to avoid scratching when it is used inside a carcass. All abrasives lose some of their grit through use; it just falls off and becomes mixed up with the dust being made. If the surface is not dusted before moving to a finer grade, particles of larger grit (a) may become embedded underneath the finer paper and will continue repeatedly to put the same depth of scratch into the surface. You may think you are using a finer grade but the reality is quite different.

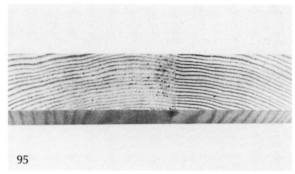

95

(95) The most important guide of all is to look for clarity of grain markings. The grain on the left of the photograph is fuzzy and should be cleaned up until the grain markings are crisp and clear.

(96) On end grain, look for clear, distinct annual rings or medullary rays. Any fuzziness will normally mean that a little more work is needed with the block and paper. The end grain on a piece of oak (*see* photograph) will show up every detail when cleaned up properly.

96

(97) On sides and edges, look for light patches. As with tears, these are rough surfaces filled with dust and need special attention. You can never do too much final finishing. It is knowing when to stop each stage which will keep the work to a minimum.

97

(98) Make a decision as to the finish you intend to use before cleaning up. A natural colour finish does not require such attention to detail as when you intend to stain the wood. If you are going to stain, the least scratch will go black when the stain is applied because it will take up much more colour. This applies to both light and dark stains.

The higher the gloss you intend to use, the more thorough the cleaning up will need to be. If you are looking for a mirror finish, such as that on a grand piano or a highly polished dining table, the surface must be absolutely blemish-free. The least chip or scraper mark will show up like a ripple on otherwise calm water, the only difference being that the water ripple will eventually recede and fade away, but the scraper mark will be visible for ever.

Satin or lustre finishes will allow a few errors and still give a 'nice' finish. A matt surface will provide the most

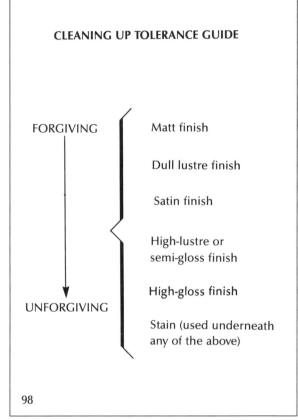

CLEANING UP TOLERANCE GUIDE

FORGIVING → Matt finish

Dull lustre finish

Satin finish

High-lustre or semi-gloss finish

High-gloss finish

UNFORGIVING → Stain (used underneath any of the above)

98

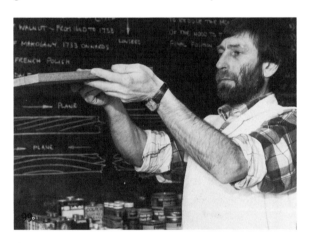

forgiving finish of all, when new. You must bear in mind, though, that subsequently the piece being finished may collect dirt in the tears and these will show up after the piece of furniture has been in use for a while.

(99) For cleaning up, it is important to use touch and sight in unison. Run your fingertips lightly over the surface to detect a ripple mark. If the piece of wood is small enough, hold it up to a light source and sight it at a low angle to see the same ripple. Different lights will show up marks not previously noticed, so take it to a window and look again.

(100) For larger work on the bench, you must bend down and sight the piece from different directions; scratches will be spotted only by close examination of the surface. If the lighting in your workshop is poor, consider using a desk lamp to inspect the surface.

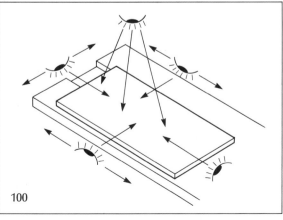

100

(101) When cleaning up flat boards, the use of abrasives is straightforward enough – simply follow the rule of keeping to the direction of the grain. This becomes more difficult when two or more pieces of wood are glued together with a mitre, for example, in the case of a picture frame. It is impossible not to run the glass-paper across the grain, so work through the appropriate grades of paper going round the frame with each grade. Try to finish off with each grade by papering around the corner, and be sure to use a block. Each grade must remove the scratches of the previous grade. Finish with flour paper.

(102) On a frame where the shoulders are at right angles instead of at 45 degrees, work on the short sides first. This will make scratches across the grain of the other pieces (a) which are taken out at the second stage. Work through the grades of paper using both stages for each grade. Keep working the second stage on each grade until the scratches for that grade are removed. You

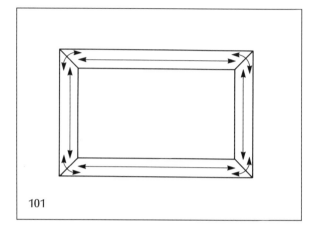

101

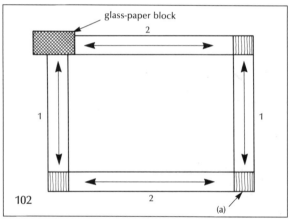

102

will need to line the block up carefully to the shoulder or further scratches will be made. Finish with flour paper.

(103) The above method should also be used on more complicated framing and on the edges of carcasses.

(104) The method of cleaning up curved surfaces will depend on how close to the line you have managed to cut and how even it is. If you have used a coping saw, then a spokeshave (a) will probably have to be used to clean off the lumps. Work with the grain as much as possible to give the best finish. If you have used a band-saw or have managed to cut evenly with a coping saw, then 60-grit aluminium oxide wrapped round either a curved (b) or a flat (c) glass-paper block will remove small lumps very efficiently. Using the same-shaped block, work through finer grades of paper, finishing with flour paper as previously described.

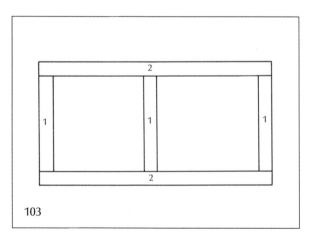

103

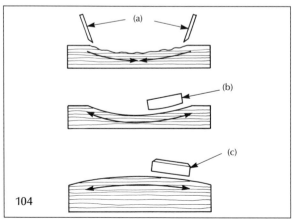

104

(105) For shaped edges, it is just as important to avoid using your fingers as it is on flat surfaces. The edges of mouldings should be left crisp, but not sharp. Shaped softwood blocks with abrasives wrapped tightly around them do not take long to make, and their efficiency will more than recover the time spent making them. You must not forget to dust out mouldings before moving to a finer grade of paper.

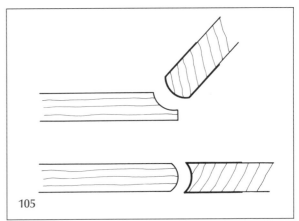

105

(106) For curves with a small radius where spokeshaves cannot be used, you will find that smooth files of a suitable cross-section will work well. It is important to slide the file from side to side along the curve at the same time as pushing it backwards and forwards. This will give a smoother, more flowing curve. If you use only backward and forward strokes, you will tend to produce a curve equal in radius to that of the file profile.

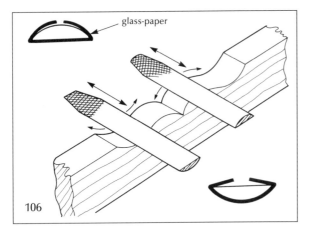

glass-paper

106

(107) To remove file marks and obtain a suitable surface for finishing, you will need to wrap abrasive paper tightly around the file and use the same action as before. If you have used a smooth file, then 120 glass-paper followed by flour paper will normally suffice. Before moving to a finer grade of paper, work along the grain following the shape of the edge. This removes the scratches made whilst using the paper across the grain.

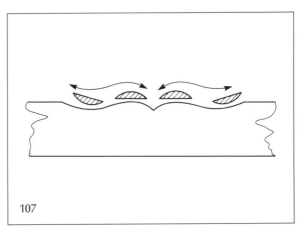

107

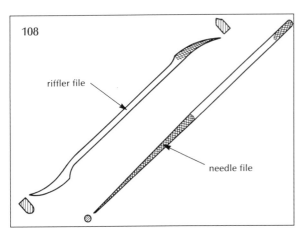

108

riffler file

needle file

(108) For carved work and more intricate edging, you may find that ordinary files are too large. In this case, it is useful to have a set of needle files. These are available in a range of cross-sectional shapes and are invaluable if you intend to do some restoration work. They may be used on their own or with fine abrasive papers wrapped around them. Also available are riffler files, which are curved at the ends and which also have different cross-sectional shapes.

(109) Scraping and the correct use of abrasives with a block will leave corners which are extremely sharp. You must dull these off before applying the finish. There are two reasons for this: first, sharp corners can cause nasty cuts. During construction and finishing you can sensibly avoid this but give consideration to the way in which the article will be treated in the home. It will be dusted and polished, meaning that fingers and hands will come into contact with the corners with both speed and pressure. This is when cuts are most likely to occur. It is even more important if you are making children's toys.

109

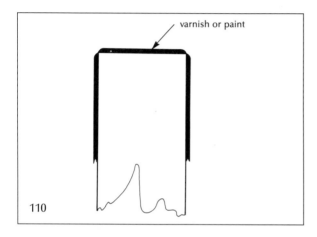

varnish or paint

110

(110) The second reason for removing sharp corners is that finishes do not adhere to them readily, especially those applied with a brush – for example, varnishes and lacquers. These tend to lie on the surface, unlike oils and waxes which soak in. This is particularly important when preparing surfaces for external work. Painted or varnished doors and window frames begin to show the effects of weather at sharp corners first. The finish lifts at the corner allowing water to seep underneath.

(111) The removal of sharp corners is best done with a fine abrasive wrapped tightly around a block. The best grade to use is 120 glass-paper. It must be emphasized that you should not normally try to round the corners, but merely dull them off. A couple of light strokes are sufficient, followed by a couple of strokes with flour paper.

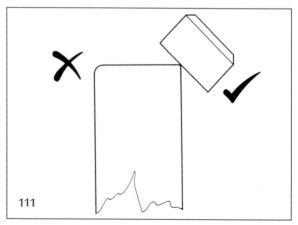

111

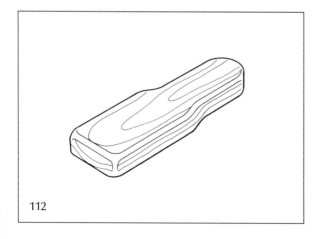

112

(112) Of course, there are occasions when corners are deliberately rounded, such as the edges on the seat of a rocking horse. In this case, the radius would be worked with a plane and then cleaned up in the normal way.

Dulling off the corners is the very last stage in the cleaning process.

Machine Sanders

You may have noticed that my procedure for cleaning up does not include machine sanders. They do create a lot of dust even when fitted with a dust bag or vacuum cleaner, and the noise from sander and cleaner does not make for enjoyable woodworking. The main reason, though, is simply that they do not do an efficient job.

(113)   There are three main types of sanding machine; disc, belt and orbital finishing sanders. It is vital when using all abrasives that you work with the grain, but by its design the disc sander cannot achieve this. Even when tipped on to one edge and with a flexible pad, it will leave deep scratches and ridges.

(114)   Belt sanders do work with the grain, but they are not normally wide enough to cover the entire surface and will tend to leave lines, however much you try to keep them on the move.

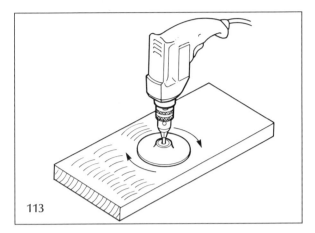

113

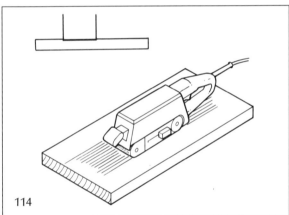

114

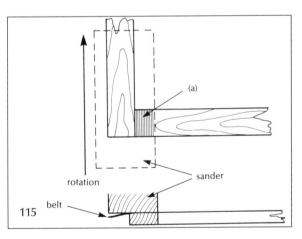

(a)

rotation

sander

115   belt

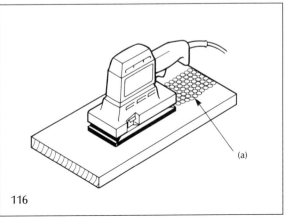

116

(a)

(115)   Used on frames, a belt sander tends to make scores (a) across the adjacent piece of the frame, and if the belt is slightly loose or worn then edges and corners will be rounded off.

(116)   Orbital sanders are the least likely to cause damage, but the problem of dubbing over the edges still remains. By their very nature, they sand the surface in small circles and leave small, round scratches (a). These must be removed by hand afterwards, and are more difficult to remove than you would think. Orbital sanders are very slow at removing tears and other marks.

The cost of keeping these machines supplied with the correct discs, belts or sheets is another good reason for not using them, not to mention their initial cost. As a rough comparison, a new cabinet scraper, which will last a lifetime, costs about the same as ten discs or three belts or sixteen sheets of ready-cut paper – the machines therefore are hardly cost-effective.

In addition to the three main types, there are drum sanders and flap wheels. These are both used with an electric drill as the power base.

(117) Drum sanders consist of an abrasive belt which is placed around a foam drum. They do have the advantage of working with the grain, but on wide surfaces the least tipping will create ridges.

(118) On normal edges, the softness of the foam will tend to give rounded edges rather than square ones. They also pose a problem on the ends of boards where corners are likely to be rounded off. The problem will arise whether the drum is taken off the end or applied to it. Exactly the same problems occur with the flap wheel **(119)**.

I have found all machine sanders to be inferior to hand finishing for cabinet work, but useful for work requiring a less exacting surface, such as general carpentry and joinery work.

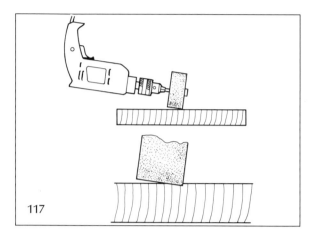

117

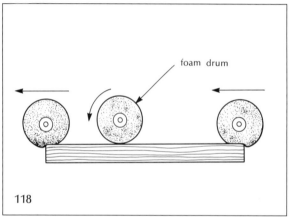

foam drum

118

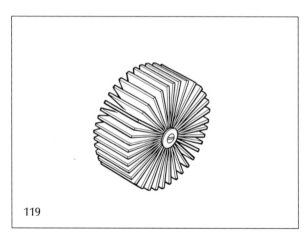

119

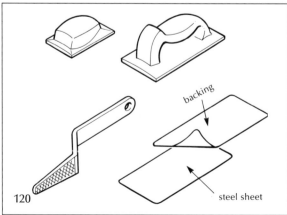

backing

steel sheet

120

(120) Before leaving the subject of sanding, mention should be made of sandplate sanders. These are a comparatively new innovation and comprise a replaceable, self-adhesive, flexible steel sheet with a peel-off backing which is either glued on to a plastic plate with a handle – rather like a file – or on to a plastic shaped block intended for use in the same way as the glass-paper block and abrasive paper. They do stay very sharp for a long time, do not clog and do remove material very efficiently. They are ideal for some projects and DIY jobs on the house. They are unsuitable for fine cabinet work since they have a limited range of equivalent grit sizes, being available in fine, medium or coarse.

If you find yourself at odds with my views on this subject, I would ask that you try the method of cleaning up suggested. I think you will find that it is more efficient, gives better results and is certainly a more pleasant form of woodworking.

Dermatitis This is the most common complaint caused by wood finishing. It occurs when the skin is exposed to a whole range of irritants such as french polishes, turpentine, thinners, wood dyes and strippers. Apply barrier cream before work starts, wear protective gloves and wash hands thoroughly when finished.

Dust The finer particles of dust produced by both machine and hand sanding wood can cause nasal cancer. The risk is not confined to wood dust but is also increased by fumes from sealers and fillers, and by dust from abrasive papers and steel wool. There is also a risk of dust explosions when fine dust is suspended in the air near an ignition source. Wear a face mask **(121)** and ensure your workshop has good ventilation. Use a vacuum cleaner to remove dust from the working area. Use power sanders with an extraction system or a collection bag.

Flammable Liquids All such liquids have a flashpoint label on the manufacturer's container. The flashpoint of a product is the lowest temperature at which the vapour or fumes will be ignited by a spark or naked flame when air is present. They can be either high risk or low risk, depending on the flashpoint temperature. The higher the flashpoint, the lower the risk and the lower the flashpoint, the higher the risk. Those with a low flashpoint have a label marked: 'highly inflammable'; or 'petroleum mixture giving off inflammable heavy vapour'. The vapour in the latter will

fall to the floor and can creep towards heaters; this is particularly dangerous if you are working in a shed or garage in winter. Of course you must have warm, dry conditions for wood finishing, but remember that if you carelessly leave a lid off a container for a couple of hours and leave the heater on so that it will be nice and warm when you return you will have left a bomb on your bench. You should also give some thought to the storage of these liquids. Always work in a well-ventilated area. Do not smoke. Store all flammables in a cool place out of the sun. Large quantities should be stored outside in a metal bin with a lid, in a disused coal bunker, or in an old fridge. Make sure that the storage container can be locked if you have children or if children are likely to visit. Dispose of rags used for these liquids safely and immediately after working as per the manufacturer's instructions, and in particular those used for oil finishes. Read the label on the tin carefully.

General Advice Consider the risks for each finishing operation and take precautions against them. Each working environment is different. The ventilation and method of heating of your work area should be considered carefully. Storage and safe disposal of materials should take into account children and pets. Each finishing operation requires thought as to the protection of the body, and the eyes, lungs and skin in particular. Install a fire extinguisher and keep a first-aid kit in the workshop at all times **(122)**. Two words sum it up – *common sense*.

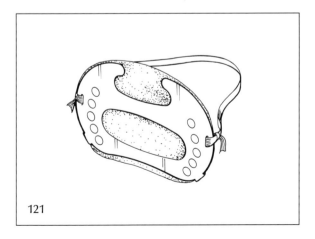

121

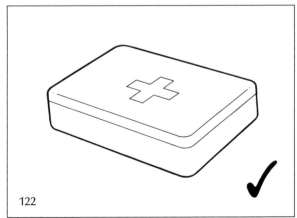

122

In an ideal world and on new work the process of filling and stopping should not be necessary, but you should remember that wood is a natural material and is not always perfect, and neither are we. To put this into perspective, I always cite the example of a concert pianist who performs for three hours without anyone noticing his playing a wrong note – he is a master of disguise. A craftsman must use his or her skill in a similar way – on a project that may have taken many, many hours, everyone is bound to have made mistakes. That is not to say, however, that you should approach the job with the attitude 'It doesn't matter, I can always fill it'. Nothing looks worse than work plastered with filler. With a little initiative, there is often a better way of masking an error.

I was once fitting a pine kitchen that had a top hingeing door over the oven unit and, foolishly, I drilled a hole for the handle at the top. I could have used filler, but even with a good choice of colour it would have been

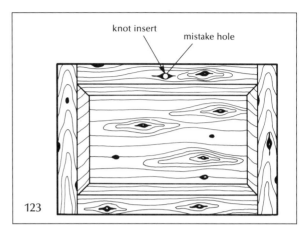

123

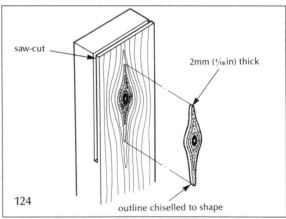

124

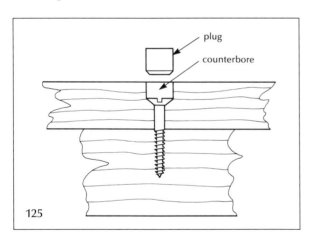

125

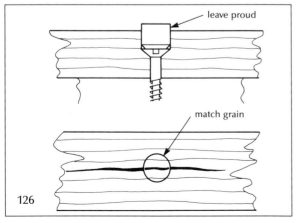

126

obvious. I opted instead to cut a 2mm ($\frac{1}{16}$ in) thick knot insert from a piece of scrap. I scribed round it on the door, carefully chiselled out a recess to suit and glued it in place – it looked like just another knot **(123)(124)**. Use filler as a last resort, and consider other alternatives first.

Covering screws with filler is quite acceptable for a painted finish; if the work is to be polished, then a better method is to counterbore the hole and use a plug of the same material as the rest of the work **(125)**. Special plug cutters are available for this purpose. The plug should be glued in place with the grain running in the same direction to match, as far as possible, the surrounding wood. Leave it slightly proud of the surface so that you can clean it off when set **(126)**.

If you must use a filler – we all do from time to time – there are four main types to choose from.

Wax Filler Sticks

Known as beaumontage, these are made from carnuba wax, resin and powdered colours. They can be used in three ways. Warmed slightly by cutting off a piece and kneading it between your fingers, it can be used as a putty, pushing it into holes and cracks with the blade of a knife (127). For a small crack, they can be rubbed vigorously at right angles to the crack, rather like rubbing out a pencil line on paper (128). They can also be melted and run into the defect with a soldering iron (129). For most filling operations, the latter is the best method as long as the work can be laid horizontally. It is generally stated that the sticks are not suitable for use under french polish, but I have found no difficulty, as long as a rubber and not a brush is used for applying the polish.

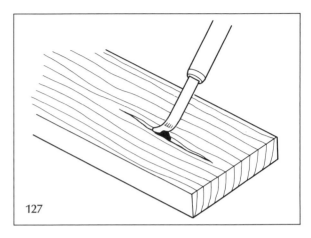

127

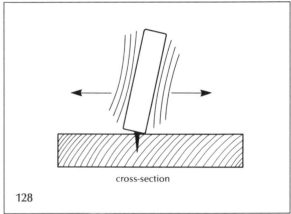

cross-section

128

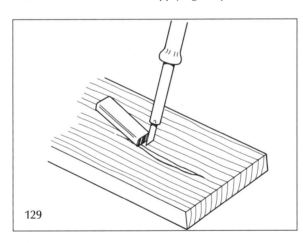

129

Shellac Filler Sticks

These are also known as beaumontage and are specifically made for use under french polish finishes because, as the main ingredient for french polish is shellac, it is therefore compatible with the filler. They are very hard and must be melted into the defect with a hot tool. Both types of filler sticks are available in a wide range of colours. A typical range would be pine, oak, middle oak, walnut, brown mahogany, red mahogany, rosewood, teak, Jacobean oak and ebony. Shellac filler sticks are also available in white and transparent. They can be intermixed in their molten state for an exact colour match if you are willing to take the time, but you should take care not to melt them over a naked flame. If melted into a hole or crack, they tend to shrink on cooling. You should, therefore, build them up full to stand proud, and either scrape or glass-paper back to the surface (130).

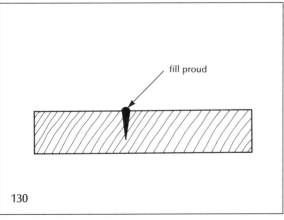

fill proud

130

(131) If you want to build up a corner using beaumontage (a), then it is necessary to build up a wall of sticky tape or masking tape (b) first. Melt the stopping with a soldering iron (c) into the corner slightly above the level required and remove the tape when it has set. The same method can be used for edges and is useful in restoration work. Remember when using these stoppers that they do not take stain and the colour should match the chosen colour of the stain you intend to use. It is vital to check this on spare timber of the same type and colour before using both filler and stain if a perfect match is to be realized.

Brummer Stopping

This is best described as an extremely stiff paste which is applied with a knife. It is available in two grades – interior and exterior – and is available in a wide range of colours which may be intermixed for a good match and which can also be mixed with stains. It dries somewhat lighter than when first applied so checking is important once again. It tends to be brittle and is best avoided on corners and edges. It also takes time to harden, whereas beaumontage hardens almost instantly.

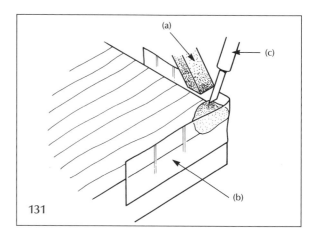

131

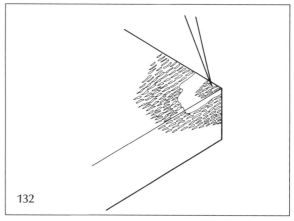

132

FILLING AND STOPPING ADVICE

- Avoid them if possible
- Think carefully about the alternatives – use filler only as a last resort
- Fill above the final level and smooth off
- Clean off thoroughly, especially around filled areas and especially if staining
- Check colour of filler sticks with intended stain, or wood when it is dry or set
- Texture the surface if the final finish has an open grain
- Do not melt filler sticks with a naked flame

THE FOUR MAIN TYPES OF FILLER ARE:

- Wax filler sticks (Beaumontage)
- Shellac filler sticks (Beaumontage)
- Brummer stopping
- Plastic wood

133

Plastic Wood

This is convenient to use as it comes in tubes, but it is not really a craftsman's product. It has the advantage that it is petroleum-based and, therefore, hardens quickly in shallow blemishes. Deeper defects need to be filled using several thin layers or it will remain soft underneath for a long time. It does not take stain readily, and unless the area around the filled defect is cleaned really thoroughly it will leave a light patch when you apply the stain.

(132) You must always be aware of the fact that when cleaned off, all fillers and stoppers will be completely smooth. They have no openness of grain or pores. If you intend to have an open-grained finish, it is important to disguise the filler by introducing 'open grain' into the filler surface by scoring carefully with a marking knife or scriber.

(134) Filling the grain should not be confused with filling or stopping, which is for cracks, holes and other blemishes. Filling the grain involves filling the pores in the wood, these being the channels along which the sap flowed when the tree was growing. Some trees – generally hardwoods – produce open-grained timber; ramin, mahogany, oak, ash and elm are examples. Softwoods do not normally need to be filled.

(135) It is important to understand that grain filling is not an essential part of the finishing process. It is purely a matter of choice. You have to decide whether or not you want a 'full' finish. This is one where all the grain is filled completely to give a mirror finish, or 'piano' finish as it is sometimes called. Fullness of grain is normally associated with a high gloss, but you can fill the grain under a matt or satin lustre if you want to. Personally I much prefer to see the texture of the wood, since that is part of its beauty, but very often the customer or the actual nature of the work will dictate the need for full grain.

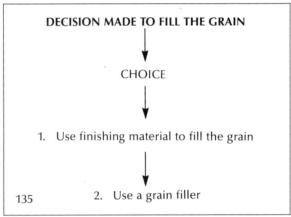

134

a full grain

level surface

grain left open

finishing material

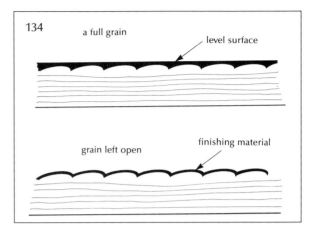

DECISION MADE TO FILL THE GRAIN

CHOICE

1. Use finishing material to fill the grain

135

2. Use a grain filler

If full grain is required, there are two routes to achieve the same result. The first is to fill the grain gradually with the chosen finish, and the second requires the use of a ready-made grain filler as a separate process.

(136) Filling the grain with the finishing material is done by applying successive coats and cutting back between each coat. The cutting back is done with very fine abrasive paper such as flour paper, but take care not to rub back to bare wood. Each coat will fill the grain a little more whilst the surface level will remain more or less the same. The sequence of diagrams shows just four coats, but in practice it may require many more.

Applying many coats of a finish may lengthen the whole finishing process considerably, especially if you need to allow several hours for each coat to harden – as with varnish.

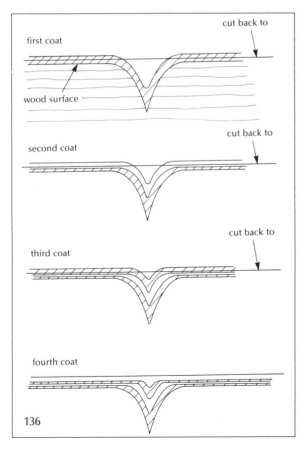

first coat

cut back to

wood surface

second coat

cut back to

third coat

cut back to

fourth coat

136

(137) When using this method, you should completely fill the grain with finish (a) to your satisfaction and then set the work aside for several days to allow the finished surface to harden and settle.

(138) As the finishing material shrinks as it hardens, it may cause 'sinking' (a) and some openness of grain may become apparent again. When this happens, you should apply more coats of the finish, rubbing down between each as before. Only when you are certain that all sinking has stopped can you be sure that the grain is completely filled. For all the extra time involved and the possible problem of sinking, this method of filling the grain is still considered by many to be superior to using grain fillers.

(139) Grain fillers normally fill the grain completely in one application, although on very open timbers a second coat is sometimes needed. They can be obtained as a powder, paste or thick liquid and are

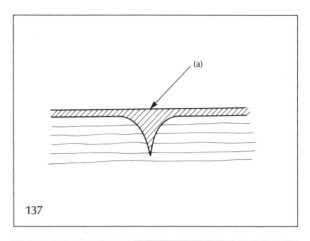

137

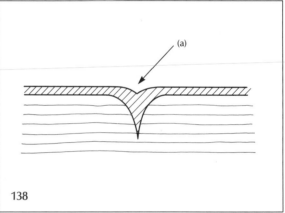

138

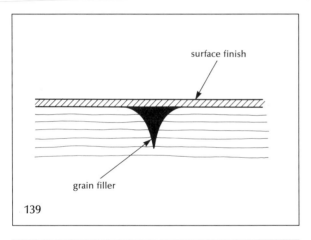

139

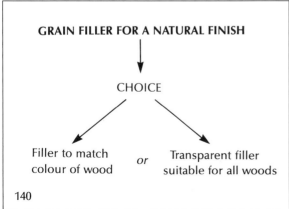

140

available in a wide range of colours to suit the work in hand. A typical range would be light, natural, medium and dark oak, light and medium mahogany, light and medium walnut, cedar and teak. The colours can be intermixed to obtain an exact shade to match the wood, but I advise you only to mix those made by the same manufacturer.

(140) For a natural finish – in other words, one without stain – it is a simple matter of using a filler which, when dry, is of a compatible colour to that of the wood. I must stress *when dry*, since the fillers do change colour as they dry out – always check on a spare piece of the same wood first.

An alternative is to use a transparent grain filler. This is a thick liquid which has the consistency of, and is about the same colour as syrup, and which will suit all woods. Because it is a liquid, it generally requires a second application.

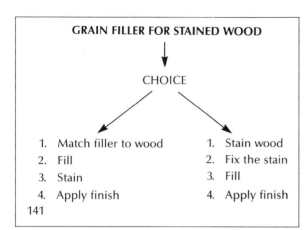

GRAIN FILLER FOR STAINED WOOD

CHOICE

1. Match filler to wood	1. Stain wood
2. Fill	2. Fix the stain
3. Stain	3. Fill
4. Apply finish	4. Apply finish

141

(141) If you intend to stain the wood, you could use a filler that matches bare wood, then fill the grain, stain and finish as required. Alternatively, stain the wood first and apply a coat of shellac sealer to fix the stain. Apply filler to match the stained colour and then proceed with the finishing. The main difficulty you may find in using this method is that when cutting back the hard excess filler you may go back to bare wood, especially on corners and mouldings. The rule of checking your planned approach on spare timber still applies.

Some fillers will stain and fill the grain at the same time, while others can be mixed with stain to achieve the same result.

(142) The method of applying the filler is the same no matter which type is used. If you are using a powder, it can either be mixed to a paste first or put on with a damp rag to give the same effect. Apply the filler with a piece of coarse cloth: hessian or denim is ideal. Use circular movements first of all, and apply a fair amount of pressure because you are trying to push the filler into the grain. Tickling the surface will trap air underneath and will cause the filler to sink later. Take special care to work the edges and ends as these always tend to be missed.

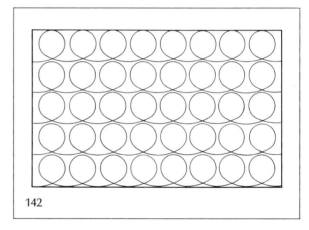

142

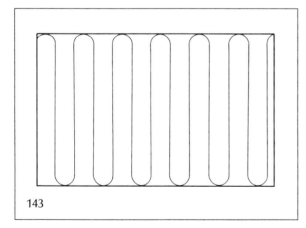

143

(143) Finish off with straight strokes across the grain and leave to dry.

(144) When the filler has hardened (preferably over-night) you should cut back with fine abrasive paper to remove all excess filler. Work with the grain, paying particular attention to internal corners. How much filler to apply will be determined with practice; too much will make hard work of cutting back and too little will necessitate a second application. All fillers shrink a little on hardening.

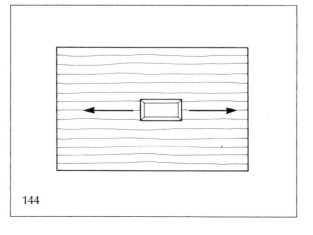

144

(145) Staining is done for three reasons: first, it makes one wood look like another; second, it makes a piece of new furniture match existing items; and third, it enhances the grain of some woods.

Given the choice of staining the wood or leaving it a natural colour, I would always choose the latter. Wood is available in a vast range of colours and if you are able to select one that will give you the effect you want without staining then I advise you to take that course of action. Over the years, I have seen really wonderful pieces of furniture made and then spoiled by a desire to stain them. This is why it is so important to consider the finishing early on, before buying your wood. It is of little use to buy pine and then, at a later stage, try to imitate mahogany. It simply will not work. Even discounting the knots, the grain pattern is so markedly different that you are bound to be disappointed with the result. If you want your piece of work to look like mahogany, then buy mahogany.

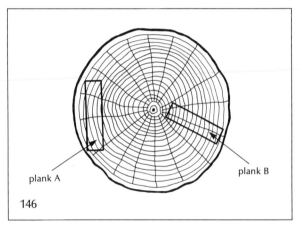

STAINING IS NECESSARY TO

↓

Make one type of wood look like another

↓

To shade the wood to match existing furniture

↓

To enhance certain grain characteristics

145

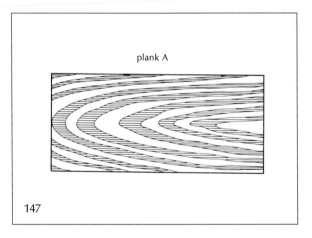

plank A

147

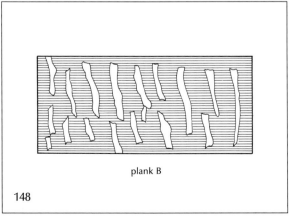

plank B

148

I have chosen mahogany as my example here because I can foresee a problem in future years. With green issues to the fore, you may be opposed to buying it. The price may become prohibitive or the supply may cease altogether. If and when this becomes the case, staining will be a necessity if you want mahogany-coloured furniture. Using alternative types of wood and then colouring them is already common practice in mass-produced furniture. This is not done by staining the wood though; instead the wood is sprayed with the colour incorporated in the finishing material. Successful disguise is dependent on a good choice of alternative wood. For mahogany, ramin, abura or jelutong are good choices, although the latter is a little soft. Each has a similar grain structure and takes stain well.

(146) Shows two planks with different grains.
(147) Shows how stain can enhance the annual rings.
(148) Shows how stain can enhance silvering caused by medullary rays, especially in oak.

Figure 146 caption:

plank A

plank B

146

Whatever your reason for staining, it should never be regarded as an easy option. As seen earlier, surface preparation must be perfect because the least scratch will show as a black line and each area of glue will show as a light patch. Great care is needed in its application if a professional finish is to be achieved.

(149) The greatest difficulty you are likely to encounter in your first attempts at staining is the problem caused by end grain. To understand this, you must appreciate the structure of the wood. It comprises bundles of

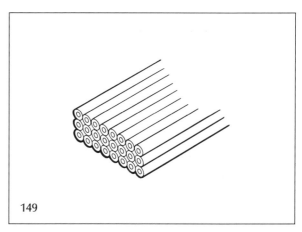

149

extremely fine tubes, the ends of which appear on the end grain. When stain is applied, it is drawn up the tubes by capillary action. This results in a much darker and sometimes almost black appearance on the ends.

(150) Take, for example, a solid oak table top, moulded along both edges and ends. If you apply stain evenly to all surfaces, the ends will be darker than the rest (a).

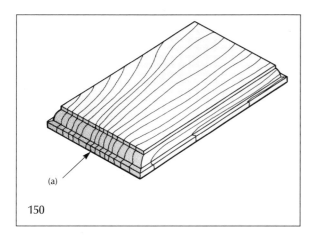

(a)

150

(151) The only way to overcome the problem is to prevent capillary action from taking place. This is done before staining by sealing off the tubes with a sealer in the form of translucent or white french polish. Both of these products are readily available in small quantities, and can be applied with a polishing rubber, a lint-free rag or with a brush.

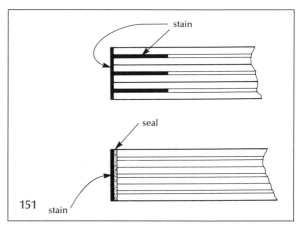

stain

seal

151   stain

(152) The sealer spreads over the top edge (a), you must cut this back to bare wood when dry. If this is not done then you will seal that area as well, the result being a light line along the edge (b) where the stain cannot penetrate as deeply as it does over the rest of the area.

On some woods and with some stains, you may need to apply a second coat of sealer. There are no hard and fast rules, but check your method on spare timber first.

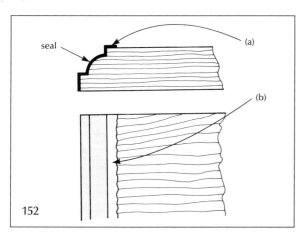

seal

(a)

(b)

152

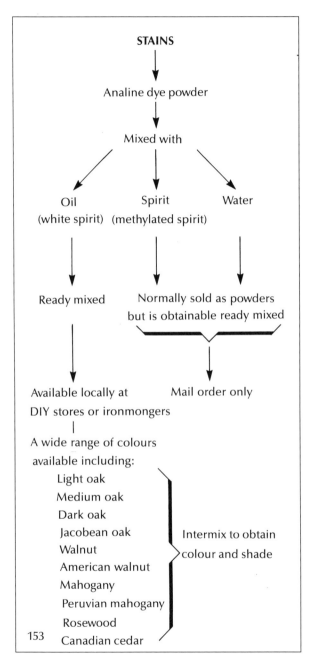

STAINS

↓

Analine dye powder

↓

Mixed with

Oil
(white spirit)

Spirit
(methylated spirit)

Water

↓

Ready mixed

↓

Available locally at
DIY stores or ironmongers

A wide range of colours
available including:

Light oak
Medium oak
Dark oak
Jacobean oak
Walnut
American walnut
Mahogany
Peruvian mahogany
Rosewood
Canadian cedar

Intermix to obtain
colour and shade

Normally sold as powders
but is obtainable ready mixed

↓

Mail order only

153

Types of Stain

(153) Stains are analine dye powders which are soluble in a liquid base. There are three main types: oil, spirit and water.

Oil Stains

These are the easiest to use and are the only ones readily available outside mail order – they are sold in shops as wood dyes. The oil base is white spirit, or sometimes a mixture of white spirit and naptha. When buying oil stains, it is of little use to purchase one tin of mahogany stain if you want a mahogany colour. It will normally be much too red, so instead you should merely regard it as the main ingredient for your stain. You will have to mix it with dark oak or walnut stain to take the redness out or, to put it more poetically, brown it down. Wood dyes are comparatively inexpensive when you consider your investment in time and materials up to this stage. To buy two or three colours in order to mix the exact shade you want is therefore well worth it, but do make sure that you only mix colours made by the same manufacturer. There is no magic recipe for obtaining the correct shade, although the professional does have two advantages: firstly experience and secondly a wide selection of tins on the shelf from which to choose. You can easily build up the latter and experience is only gained through practice – always remember that the professional still uses trial and error, although he or she will arrive at the correct recipe a little sooner.

(154) Apart from the colour of the stain being applied, there are two criteria which will affect the result: the colour of the wood itself and the colour of the finishing material. It is *vital* to check your recipe on a spare piece of the same wood as that used for the rest of the work. It is pointless checking the stain on a piece of pine when you are staining mahogany.

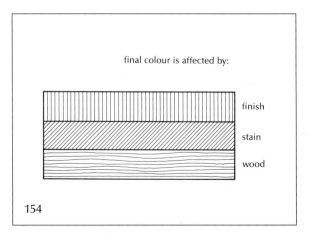

final colour is affected by:

finish

stain

wood

154

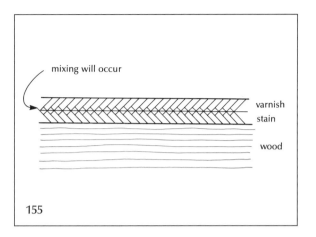

155

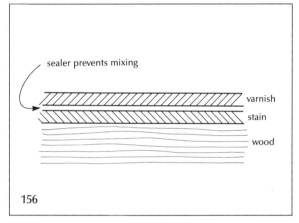

156

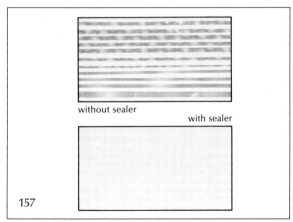

157

These stains are user-friendly and you should have little difficulty in obtaining an even finish. Leave to dry for the manufacturer's recommended time (normally about six hours) or, preferably, overnight.

Stains will normally dry lighter than when first applied and will change their appearance again when the finish is applied, though not necessarily back to the wet stain colour. Apply a coat of the intended finish to the sampler before you assume you have the effect you want. Different types of french polish and waxes can alter the tone, and if you are intending to use these as a finish then you should refer to the appropriate sections at this stage.

You can assume that the finishing material will not affect the colour after the first coat is checked if you use one of the clear finishes. These are transparent or white french polish, all the oils, light waxes and clear varnishes.

(155)(156)(157)(158) If you intend to use a varnish as a finish, whether it be matt, satin or gloss, you must seal in the stain with one coat of shellac sanding sealer or one of the french polishes (which will do the same job) before applying varnish. The reason for this is that both the oil stain and the varnish have the same base – white spirit. The varnish will cause the stain to become wet again and the brush will lift the stain into streaks of colour.

To apply the stain to the surface, it is best if you use a small piece of lint-free rag. A large piece will soak up a large quantity of stain which will be wasted when the rag is thrown away. A piece about 75mm (3in) square is ideal. It should be very wet as the stain needs to be pushed into the grain (unless this has been filled first). You should apply an even, wet coat leaving no dryish patches. Work with the grain as much as possible and avoid any tendency to streak. Wipe off any excess with a dry cloth.

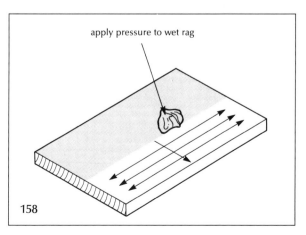

158

(159) On large surfaces it may be appropriate to apply the stain with a clean paintbrush (a) and, using a rag, to wipe off the excess (b) evenly with the grain after the whole surface has been covered. You will find that a brush is the best method when working into sharp corners, such as moulded edges or carved work.

(160) Oil stains are slightly adjustable in that some colour can be taken off with a rag dampened with white spirit (a) to make the colour slightly lighter. A second coat of the stain, applied after the first has dried, sometimes darkens it a little more. It is also possible to introduce a slightly different shade by applying a second coat of a different colour when the first has dried. However, check this on a spare piece of wood first. The process of trial and error is the only method available to achieve success. For this reason, make sure you mix enough stain of your recipe to do the entire job. It is virtually impossible to mix a second quantity which is exactly the same colour as the first.

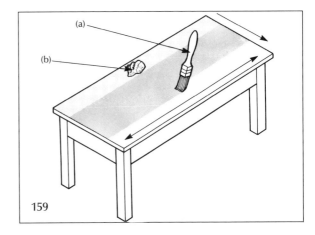

159

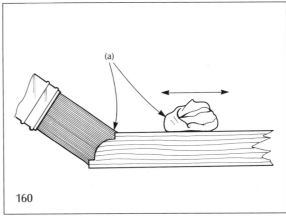

160

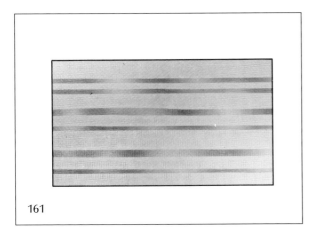

161

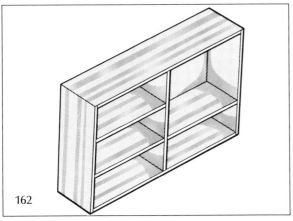

162

It is a good idea to store left-over mixes in small glass bottles. When you have another piece of work to stain, shake the bottle and hold it to the light; you will have a good idea as to the colour of its contents and will be able to use it as a base for another recipe.

Spirit Stains

(161) These are dye powders which are dissolved in a methylated spirit base. These can also be used for colouring french polishes. The problem with these stains is that they dry so quickly, and need speed and confidence in their application to maintain a wet edge. Slowness will result in a streaked appearance.

(162) You should also consider the piece of work to be stained. A beginner would have difficulty obtaining evenness of colour on a bookcase where many corners are involved; overlap would make the corners darker and give a patchy surface.

(163) Spirit stains can be purchased as a powder or as a ready-mixed liquid. They are not available in DIY stores and must be bought by mail order unless you live near one of the specialist suppliers of finishing materials.

As a powder, you buy base colours of the stain. Ready-mixed stains are described as wood colours. They can all be intermixed at will to give an endless range of shades. It is best to mix the powders with methylated spirit and store them in labelled bottles. These should be used to mix your recipe, rather than adding small quantities of powder to a mix. About ¾ of a teaspoon of powder to 150ml (5fl oz) of spirit gives an average strength stain; add more spirit if you want a weaker mix or more powder for a stronger one. Also, adding one teaspoon of french polish helps to bind the solution and makes it easier to apply the stain to the wood.

SPIRIT STAIN COLOURS	
READY MIXED	POWDERS
Light oak	Bismarck brown
Medium oak	Black
Dark oak	Blue
Walnut	Brown
Red mahogany	Green
Brown mahogany	Pink
Teak	Red
Black	Yellow
Rosewood	Mauve
Golden oak	Mahogany
Golden brown	Walnut
Jacobean	Oak
Old pine	Jacobean

163

164

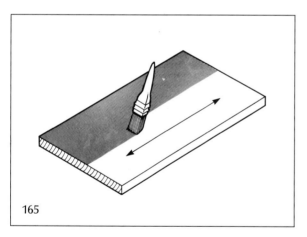

165

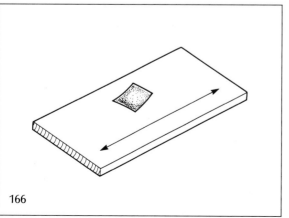

166

(164) Having mixed the stain, having made sure there is sufficient for the whole job and having fully tested for colour on spare wood of the same type, apply the stain to the surface with a brush as shown. Work with the grain and use a thin coat. You should work quickly and carefully, taking care to keep a wet edge. Overlap each brush stroke slightly. Drying time is dependent on room temperature but will normally be between five and ten minutes. This gives you plenty of time to turn the work so that you are staining on a level surface, thus making the work easier. Fast drying also allows you to apply a second coat almost straight away if you need to deepen the tone.

(165) When the stain is dry it must be fixed. This is done with a mixture of french polish and methylated spirit in about equal quantities. Apply the mixture with a brush and allow it to harden overnight.

(166) When hard, lightly go over the surface with well-worn flour paper or steel wool (0000 grade).

WATER STAIN COLOURS

READY MIXED	POWDER
Light oak	Black
Medium oak	Blue
Dark oak	Brown
Walnut/nut brown	Green
Brown mahogany (light red)	Orange
Teak	Plum red
Black	Red
Red mahogany	Silver-grey
Fumed oak	Yellow
Golden oak	Mahogany
Weathered oak	Oak
Jacobean	Walnut
Brown mahogany (light brown)	
Grey	
Yew	
Old pine	
Rosewood	
Dark rosewood	

167   *All colours may be intermixed*

1. Damp surface to raise grain

2. Cut back smooth with flour paper

3. Apply stain

4. Fix stain with shellac sealer (french polish)

168   water stain procedure

(167) Spirit stains are best for restoration work where there has been a previous finish and where there is a tendency for the surface to be a bit greasy. The base for the stain is itself a degreaser, making it take to the surface better than other stains.

Water Stains

(169) These are not as popular as they once were, mainly because of their tendency to raise the grain. If you intend to use these, it is essential that raising the grain is the last stage in the preparation process. Even then, you will find that the grain still tends to lift, but it will be reduced to a minimum. Water stains can be obtained as a powder or ready mixed, the latter containing a fixative which helps to prevent grain problems.

If the surface is rough after staining, use flour paper with a block to make it smooth. You must take great care not to cut back into the stain or it will become patchy. Extra care is needed at the ends and edges whether they are square or moulded. Water stains in powder form are best pre-mixed in bottles as for spirit stains, but allow a little time (an hour or so) for the powder to dissolve. Add a little vinegar to act as a binder; they will also benefit from the addition of a degreasing agent. A small piece of washing soda or a dash of ammonia in a pint of stain will do the job, but it is not essential.

To mix the powder colours, think of them as artists' colours in a box of paints. The effect of mixing different colours together will be the same.

Application of the stain on large surfaces is best done with a sponge or brush, so that the surface is fairly wet. Leave the stain for a couple of minutes so that it can soak in and then wipe off the excess with a dry rag. Use a brush for staining into corners and awkward mouldings, working as much as possible with the grain. Leave it to dry overnight.

Varnish Stains

(169) As their name suggests, these are varnishes with colour added. They are not suitable for cabinet work but are invaluable for windows, doors and sill boards. They are available in a wide range of colours and also in three types of finish – matt, satin and gloss. Make sure you buy an exterior variety for all outside work.

Varnish stains must be applied thinly, brushing out well to avoid streaking. Try to keep a wet edge all the time, which is not easy in hot, dry conditions. For outside decorating, try to work in the shade and use the varnish either in the morning or evening. Failure to keep a wet edge will show as a dark overlap, although thinning with white spirit helps if this is the case.

(170) Work the varnish randomly onto the surface evenly and quickly (a) and finish with straight strokes along the grain with an almost dry brush (b).

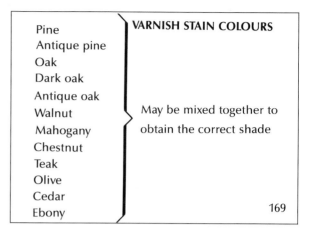

VARNISH STAIN COLOURS	
Pine	
Antique pine	
Oak	
Dark oak	
Antique oak	May be mixed together to
Walnut	obtain the correct shade
Mahogany	
Chestnut	
Teak	
Olive	
Cedar	
Ebony	169

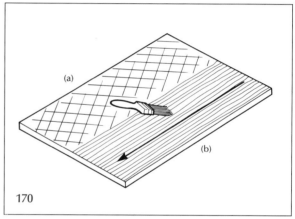

170

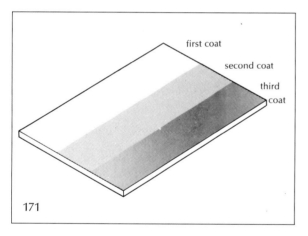

first coat

second coat

third coat

171

(171) The fact that the colour is in the varnish means that you will find each successive coat makes the colour darker, and will increasingly hide the grain **(172)**.

It is important to rub down between coats with old, worn glass-paper, 120 grit being ideal. Alternatively, use flour paper. This will remove 'nibs' caused by dust settling on the surface before the varnish is dry. After the last coat is hard, inside work can be improved if you rub down lightly with steel wool (0000 grade) and wax. Apply the wax with the wool, working with the grain. This will 'de-nib' the surface and give a very smooth finish. This method will give you a satin, or lustre, finish whether or not you have used matt, satin or gloss varnish. If you want a matt or high gloss finish, you must take care to keep dust to a minimum, as the final coat has to be left from the brush.

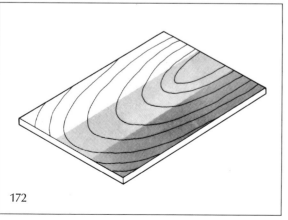

172

Wax Stains

(173) These consist of a wax base with a stain added. They can be used as a complete finish for wood but their normal use is for toning. The staining ingredient is at its most effective when applied to bare wood.

(174) These stains are best applied with a rag and worked vigorously into the surface with circular movements, pushing the wax well into the grain. Work on a small area at a time, finishing each by rubbing with the grain **(175)**.

Give the solvents a chance to evaporate (leave for ten to fifteen minutes) then buff up with the grain. Apply successive layers of wax to build up a finish. Because the surface has not been sealed, you will find that if it is left for a day or two the wax will sink into the surface and you will need to repeat the procedure. Wax stains used for toning are applied on top of another finish.

WAX STAIN COLOURS	
Limed oak	Teak
Light oak	Walnut
Medium oak	Cold walnut
Dark oak	Light walnut
Jacobean oak	Old pine
Fumed oak	Antique pine
Nut brown	Dark antique pine
Light grey	Brown mahogany
Dark grey	Red mahogany

173

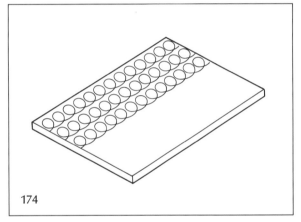

174

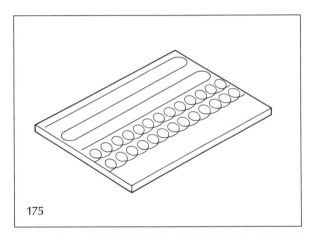

175

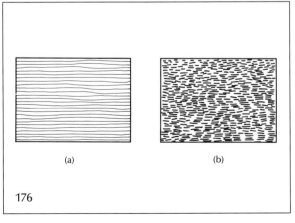

(a) (b)

176

Make sure that this finish is hard and not just dry. Waxes can be applied to all other finishes, but because the surface is sealed, the staining ingredient in the wax is less effective since it cannot penetrate the wood surface. What it does is to fill the grain with coloured wax, thus giving the appearance of a darker surface. Obviously, if the grain has been filled previously with either filler or the finishing material, then wax stains will have a negligible effect on the colour of the work. If you are dealing with mouldings or carved work, and want to avoid a build-up of dark wax in the corners, it is best to work the wax into these with a fairly soft boot or toothbrush. Darker corners can give a more antique appearance on restoration work, and when this is required the wax is best applied with a rag. Leave it to harden and then buff up with a soft brush.

(176) Shows finished work with an open grain (a) and grain filled with wax stain (b).

General Advice on Staining

Always remember that staining can irrevocably change a piece of furniture. If it is applied to work which has already been glued up, it will be impossible to remove. Include the staining in your thought processes at the design stage. A stain is more likely to enhance the work if it is a planned operation, so regard it as being just as crucial as the joints which hold the piece together.

(177) To emphasize the point, all panels (which should always be left free to move within a frame) need to be stained and preferably finished before gluing. If this is not done, you will find that subsequent movement will show a light line around the edge of the panel (a) where the stain and finish have not reached.

(178) The inside edges of frames which will receive glass should also be finished before gluing (a). Make a decision as to whether or not you are seeking to

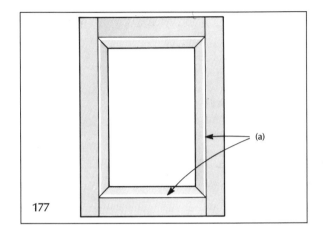

177

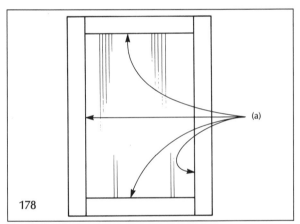

178

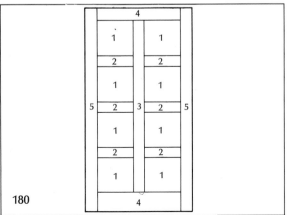

179

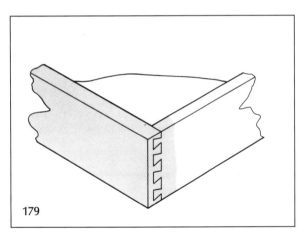

180

broaden your experience of wood finishing, or simply to give a nice finish of the right colour to a piece of furniture you have made. If the latter is the case, then my advice would be to use wood dyes. They are easily obtainable, cheap, ready mixed and you can, with experimentation, obtain the exact colour you want. To make up spirit and water stains from basic colours, experiment with a box of paints and a piece of paper. Mix a couple together and add a touch of another colour to see what the change is. The same colour stains pre-mixed in bottles and mixed together in the same combinations will give the same colour change to the stain. The two factors that determine successful staining are thorough preparation and a complete check on your planned route to the finish you are looking for.

Two examples are given: **(179)** shows the method in which drawer sides should be stained and polished; **(180)** shows the stages of applying varnish to an existing panelled door.

SATIN VARNISH – LIST OF REQUIREMENTS

1. Grain filler (optional)
2. Stain (optional)
3. Shellac sealer (if staining)
4. Clear interior varnish
5. Clean paintbrush
6. Flour paper
7. Grade 0000 steel wool
8. Wax polish (ordinary wax furniture polish)
9. Polishing Cloth

Note   Shellac sealer will adversely affect the heat
         resistance of the finish.

181

A Beautiful, Easy Finish

A satin finish is one which you can easily achieve and which, with a little care, will give a superb satin lustre in any colour or shade. Furthermore, it is hard wearing and spillage-resistant, and will take hot, wet cups without leaving ring marks, although oven dishes and hot plates are best put on mats. It will keep a good finish with normal household polishes, including aerosols. I have used it on many commission pieces, as well as pieces in my own home. When it has been done well, students have achieved top examination grades with it; I cannot give further recommendation. Try it for yourself on a small sampler first. The basis for the finish is satin varnish, although matt or gloss will give similar results. Like all finishes, varnish will not cover up poor workmanship or blemishes left from insufficient preparation. Remember that staining will highlight blemishes, while a natural finish is more forgiving.

Step 1
Fill and stain the wood if these stages are included in your plan. If you use oil stain, seal it with at least one coat of shellac sealer and de-nib when hard.

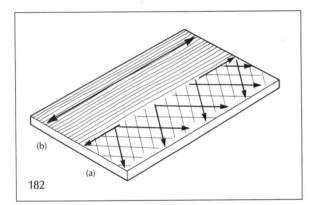

(b)

(a)

182

Step 2
(182)   Apply a thin coat of varnish. Use a brush which is almost dry, working off the edges and ends to avoid runs (a). Lay off with the grain (b) and leave to harden.

Step 3
(183)   De-nib the first coat with old, worn flour paper held in your fingers. Only work long enough to smooth the surface (a). Use a double layer of flour paper and fold it tightly to fit into the corners (b).

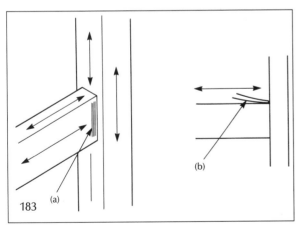

(b)

(a)

183

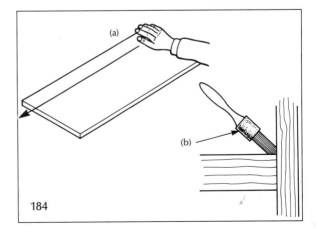

(a)

(b)

184

(184)   Dust off the surface. For large surfaces, such as table tops, use the palm of your hand (a) making straight strokes from one end to the other. Wipe your hand on your apron after each pass. For rails and corners, use a dusting brush, with the ferrule padded (b) to avoid scratches. Apply a second coat of varnish thinly. Leave to harden.

Step 4

De-nib the second coat. Apply a third. Leave to harden.

Step 5

Do not de-nib the third coat with flour paper but use steel wool and wax together, applying some pressure along the grain. Cover all the surface, paying attention to the edges and ends which tend to be missed. Buff up with a soft cloth to give a tactile finish.

(185) To work wax into the corners, use a sharpened piece of softwood with a pad of steel wool (a) wrapped over the end. After the initial waxing, you can put on as many coats of wax as you wish. To darken the tone a little, use one of the wax stain polishes. For a slightly higher gloss, use a hard finishing wax. The biggest drawback with this process is the time needed for the varnish to harden between coats. Most will dry in about six hours but this is dependent on working conditions, and it is best to leave it overnight. There is a difference

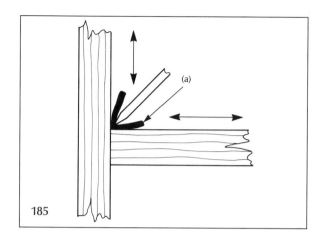

185

between being dry and being hard. An adjustable, loose shelf in a bookcase with varnish on both sides could take six days, although you can halve this time if you varnish one side early in the morning and the other late in the evening.

(186) There are alternatives. On small pieces of work, the bottom surface can be varnished first (a). Holding the edges, turn the work over and stand on four drawing pins. Varnish the top (b) and the edges (c).

(187) Run a brush or your finger under the work at the edges before you leave it. This will spread out the 'run-under'.

(188) On larger pieces, nails of equal height through a piece of batten will work well (a). Make sure the nails are the same height. Neither the drawing pins nor the nails leave perceptible marks after the wax and steel wool treatment.

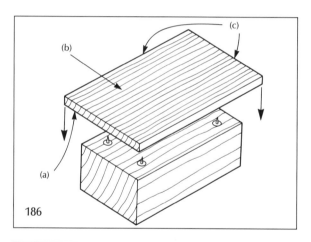

186

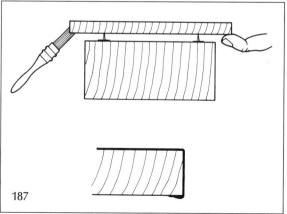

187

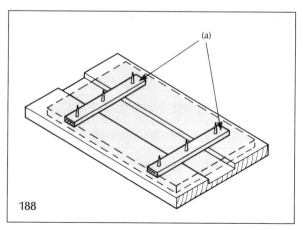

188

(189) For much larger surfaces, such as wardrobe doors, the work can be supported on battens which have sharpened edges. Place them in a different position for each coat and take out any marks when de-nibbing.

After the third coat, you may need to give an extra rub with flour paper before using steel wool. Although the de-nibbing at each stage prevents a build-up of bits in the finish, it is important to work in an environment which is as dust-free as possible. Avoid the obvious, such as sweeping the workshop just before varnishing. Organize your work so that wet varnish is left to go touch-dry before you work anywhere near it or use machines, even at some distance away. An extra stint at the workshop in the late evening ensures that the dust created during the day has settled and the work can be left overnight with no further dust being created. Before varnishing, it is worth going outside and giving your clothes a good brush to make sure that they are not full of sawdust; for this reason, it is best to work with bare arms if possible.

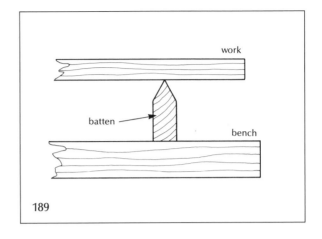

189

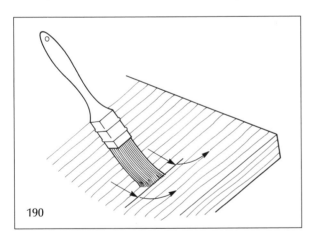

190

(190) Hairs which escape from the brush when varnishing are sometimes difficult to see, and vigilance whilst working is important. Inspect each area for bristles as you complete it and remove them while the surface is as wet as possible. Do not wait until you finish the entire job. The easiest way to remove bristles from the surface is to stab them clear with the brush. New brushes shed more bristles than old ones.

(191) Avoid runs of varnish. Check the corners and edges, and brush them out while still wet. Any brush marks should be taken out with the grain.

(192) Any runs of varnish that have been missed and left to harden must be levelled with flour paper (a) either before the next coat is applied, or before waxing if it has occurred on the final coat.

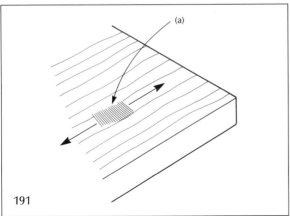

191

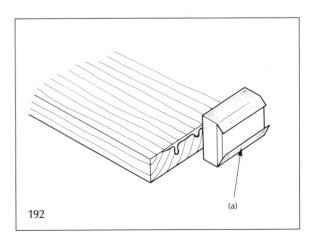

192

REQUIREMENTS FOR OIL FINISHES

Traditional Method

1. Grain filler (optional)
2. Stain (optional). **Note:** Water and spirit stains are not affected by subsequent finishing. Oil stains should be left to dry thoroughly. Some stain will be removed by the application of oil. Oil stains can be mixed with the finishing oil.
3. Oil – raw linseed or boiled linseed
4. Pure turpentine (optional). Turpentine substitute or white spirit can be used
5. Flour paper
6. Large block of wood or house brick for large surfaces
7. Soft cloth
8. Polishing board

Other Oils

1. Grain filler (optional)
2. Stain (optional). **Note:** See suitability above
3. Oil – tung, teak, Danish (Scandinavian), lemon, cedar, olive
4. Good-quality paintbrush
5. Flour paper or grade 0000 steel wool
6. Soft cloth
7. Wax polish
8. Polishing board

193

(193) An oiled finish requires no special skill in its application. It will give a finish that enhances the natural beauty of the wood, whilst giving a surface that is not affected by hot dishes or spills of hot liquids as it is impenetrable to water. Scratches due to normal wear and tear which would show up clearly on a highly polished surface are difficult to see with an oiled finish, and small blemishes which do appear can easily be polished out. All of those factors make it a very desirable finish, but it does have two distinct drawbacks which you should consider carefully before opting to use it.

The first is the time it takes to obtain a good finish. Pure linseed oil, known as raw linseed oil and obtained from the flax plant, can take up to three days to dry, depending on room temperature. You will need many applications of oil to obtain a gloss finish, although the polishing can be stopped at any stage to give a matt, satin or low gloss. The drying time can be reduced if you use boiled linseed oil. This is raw oil through which hot air has been blown and drying agents added. Boiled linseed will halve the drying time, given that the room conditions are the same.

The second point to consider is the method of applying the finish – this necessitates a little oil and a lot of elbow grease, repeated many times. The amount of rubbing makes it unsuitable where there are many corners, and a good oil finish can only really be obtained where clear surfaces are involved.

(194) If a table is taken as an example, it is really only the top (a) which requires the durability of a traditional oiled finish. For the underframe, an alternative finish which needs little or no rubbing can be used. Suitable finishes for this would be semi-wax, satin-varnish or french polish applied with a mop and cut back with steel wool to give a lustre similar to the oiled top. As long as the brightness of the finish is about the same for the whole piece it would take very close scrutiny to tell the difference between them. The advantage of durability which the oil finish gives is not really needed on most furniture and other finishes should be considered for these items.

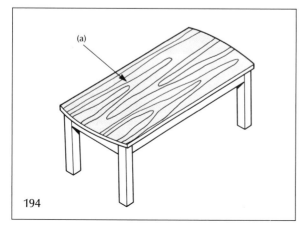

(a)

194

A linseed oil finish is unsuitable for veneered, manufactured boarding as there is insufficient thickness of wood to allow the oil to soak in properly, and for pieces made of this an alternative oil finish should be considered. There are several suitable types available; teak oil, lemon oil and tung oil. These are described in greater detail, together with their application, later in this section.

The Traditional Oil Finish

Unless you purchase your furniture from a cabinet maker and specifically ask for an oil finish, it is unlikely that new furniture will be finished in this way, because it is a time-consuming hand process. Most new items of furniture available today have various spray finishes applied to them. If you have made a one-off table, oil is certainly worth considering since you will be adding to its uniqueness. Having decided on a traditional oil finish, you then have to make a further decision as to which oil to use. The only difference is the drying time, the amount of rubbing being the same in each case.

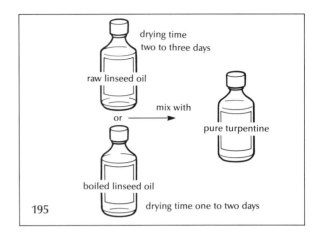

195

(195) The choice is either raw or boiled oil, used on its own or with the addition of pure turpentine to aid drying. You could use a turpentine substitute or white spirit in place of the pure turpentine if you wish, but bearing in mind the work to follow, it is satisfying to know that you have used only the purest of ingredients. A good choice and a traditional recipe is raw linseed and a one-eighth part of pure turpentine.

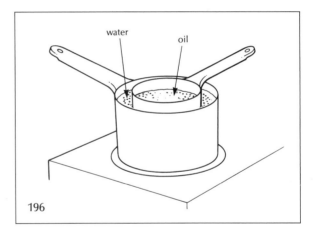

196

(196) To make the polish, simmer a known quantity of oil gently for about fifteen minutes. It is essential to use two pans for this, the outer one containing water and a smaller, inner one for holding the oil. It is also better if the bottom of the inner pan is kept clear of the outer one, allowing water to circulate underneath. Three or four pebbles or metal bottle tops will suffice. An old glue pot, as long as it is cleaned first, is ideal for small quantities.

(197) After fifteen minutes or so move the oil away from the heat source for safety and add the one-eighth measure of turpentine whilst the oil is still hot, mixing together thoroughly with a wooden stick. Leave it to cool off.

197

Finishing Method

Step 1 (Optional)

An oil finish is best applied to bare wood with the grain left open, but you can fill the grain and stain if you want a full finish or a darker colour than that of the natural wood. You can also darken the wood by using an oil stain mixed with the first couple of applications of oil if you wish. Whatever you decide, check your method on a spare piece of timber first, and remember that the oil will darken the colour of bare wood without a stain being added.

Step 2

(198) Pour some oil liberally on to a piece of cloth (a) and apply it to the wood across the grain if you have not filled it. This will push the oil into the open grain better. Finish by applying it with the grain. It is important not to flood the surface with oil but to apply a good, even coating.

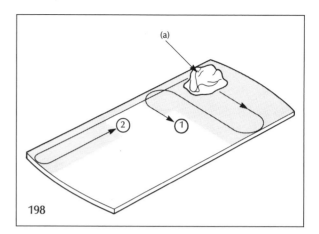

198

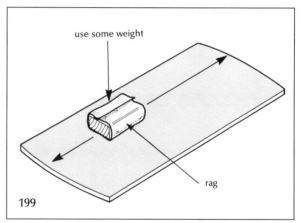

199

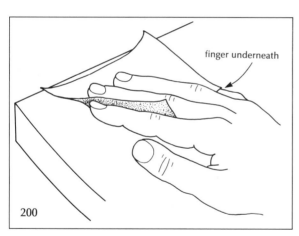

200

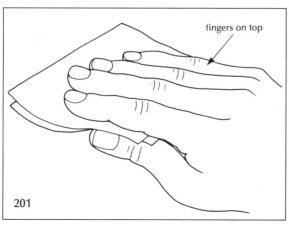

201

Step 3

(199) Rub the oil into the wood vigorously and with some pressure along the grain. A block of wood or a brick with a thick rag wrapped round it will add weight and help in the rubbing-in process. You should continue until all the oil has been worked into the surface. Do not skimp on the elbow grease as this is the basis of a good finish. Leave the work to dry for two or three days. It is best to leave it in a dust-free environment if you can. Oil finishing is ideally done in a spare room indoors, which is less dusty and warmer than most workshops, in winter especially. Warmth speeds the drying process.

Step 4

Lightly rub down the surface with flour paper held in your fingers and working with the grain. There are two methods of holding the flour paper for de-nibbing: with one finger underneath **(200)**; or with the fingers on top **(201)**. Lift off the dust with the palm of your hand or with a rag that has been very lightly dampened with turpentine.

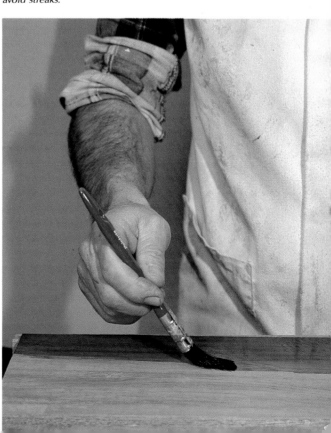

Wax filler stick being melted into a small blemish after a chair reglue.

Transparent grain filler being applied to a piece of oak.

Mixing a spirit stain with meths-soluble powders. The button polish on the right is used to fix the stain.

Applying spirit stain with a brush. Keep the edge wet to avoid streaks.

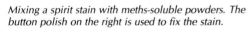

Producing a satin finish on a teak trinket box, with wax and steel wool.

A sample board of wax stains. From top to bottom: antique pine, light walnut, walnut, dark oak, Georgian mahogany. **Note** The light walnut has produced no colour change.

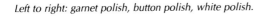

Left to right: garnet polish, button polish, white polish.

A polishing board made from off-cuts. Note the joints masked with tape to keep them free of polish.

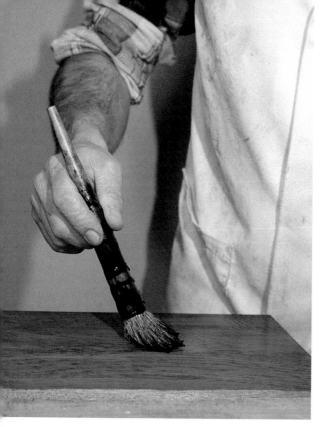

Fadding with a mop using garnet polish.

An example of colouring with French polish. The red on the piece of mahogany is being toned down with a rubber or two of green polish (right).

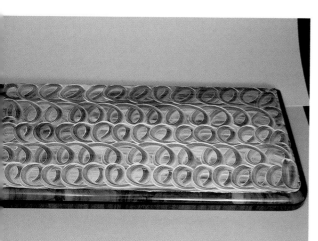

The path of a french polish rubber when using circles for bodying-up.

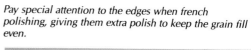

Pay special attention to the edges when french polishing, giving them extra polish to keep the grain fill even.

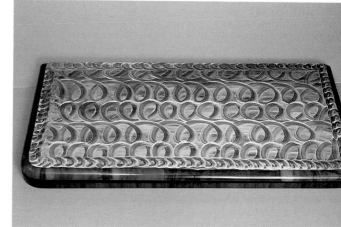

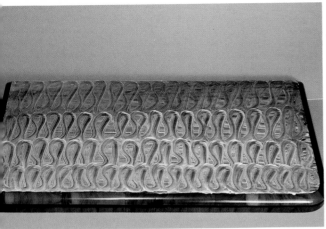

Change the path of the rubber to provide an equal thickness of French polish over the surface.

Using the polishing rubber in long loops.

Use straight strokes when the stiffing stage is reached. It can also be used in between any of the other rubber methods.

Cutting back French polish with pumice powder.

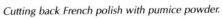

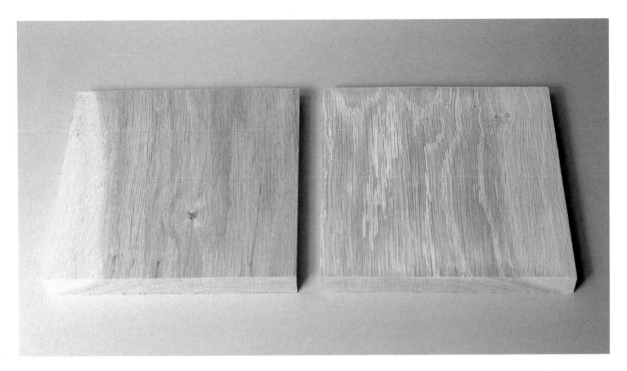

Natural oak (left) in contrast to limed oak.

Fumed oak: the sample on the left is natural, the others having been left in the fuming chamber for varying amounts of time, getting progressively darker. **Note** *Sapwood on the right sample does not change colour.*

Burning a piece of pine for a burnt and brushed finish.

Using a wire brush after burning the pine.

The texture and colour of the pine after light brushing.

The texture and colour of the pine after heavy brushing.

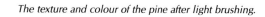

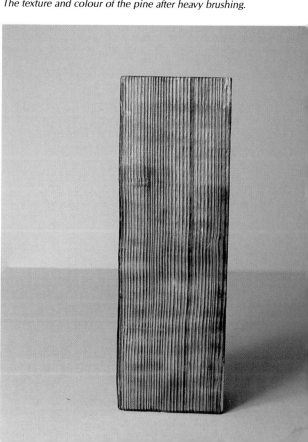

Paint stripper being applied to a table top – protect your hands and eyes.

Removing blistered paint stripper with a scraper.

A full finish on a piece of teak.

Antique finishes for pine: wax (top), natural (middle), nitric acid (bottom).

An open finish on a piece of sapele mahogany.

A matt finish.

A satin finish.

A high-gloss finish.

Step 5 Onwards

(202) Repeat Steps 2, 3 and 4 until you have reached the finish you require, which can be matt, satin or gloss. A good gloss finish will take weeks of regular applications to build a really deep shine, but will be well worth the effort. With a gloss finish, you can never really say that the finishing is complete as another application can only enhance the surface further. To maintain the finish, simply dust the surface with a dry duster as for normal house cleaning, but avoid furniture sprays and wax polishes. Occasionally, apply a thin coat of oil and rub in vigorously.

(203) If, at any time in the polishing, you find that the surface has a tendency to sweat, give it a rub down with a rag and a little methylated spirit. Leave for a day or so before applying further oil.

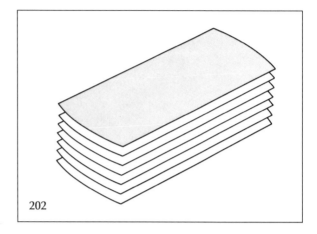

202

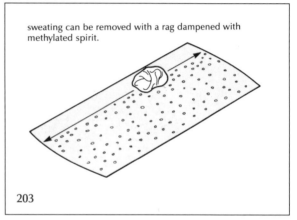

sweating can be removed with a rag dampened with methylated spirit.

203

Tung Oil Finish

This is also known as Chinese wood oil. After heat treatment, it dries faster and gives a harder film on the surface than linseed oil. It requires only two or three coats to provide a waterproof finish, but this is not as deep as linseed. On its own, it will give a very low lustre but a higher sheen can be produced if wax is applied after the last coat has hardened.

(204) This finish is ideal for the oak chest shown in the diagram. Other finishes would be equally suitable, and it is simply a matter of choice. Oil will greatly enhance and highlight the silvering effect of the medullary rays if the wood has been quarter sawn.

(205) On a project of this nature, panels should be polished before gluing up, so that any future shrinkage (a) of the wood will not show as untreated lines of bare wood round the edges (b).

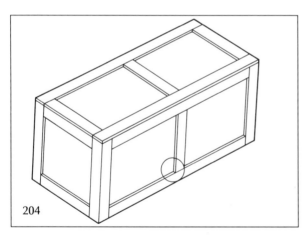

204

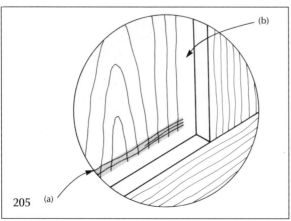

205   (a)

The inside edges of the frame are also best polished before gluing. To do them afterwards will necessitate polishing into corners, and this is difficult. The surfaces of the panels at the top and bottom are also likely to be scratched across the grain which will look unsightly.

(206) To finish the panels, you will need to hold them securely. It is best to make up a polishing board for this. The base can be of any material, and in its simplest form panels can be held by pinning thin strips of wood to the base. The panels should be a 'push fit' between the strips. If you have panels of different sizes, arrange the strips to suit the largest and use wedges to hold the smaller ones steady.

(207) To make a more versatile board, use a flat piece of any manufactured boarding at least 12mm (½in) thick. Drill a grid system of holes 9mm (⅜in) in diameter. Using dowels and wedges, work of any size can be held securely. The polishing board can be made to

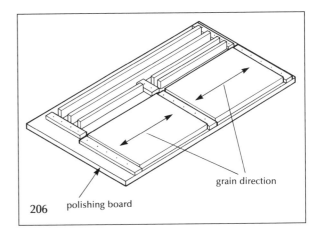

206   polishing board   grain direction

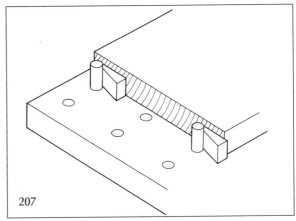

207

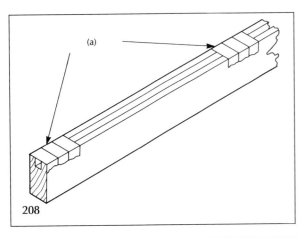

208

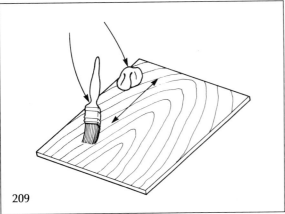

209

any dimensions, but one that can be held on the bench top without slipping is ideal.

(208) Areas of wood on the frame which are gluing surfaces should be masked off with tape (a) before polishing commences in order to keep them free of oil.

Finishing Method

Step 1 (Optional)
Fill and stain the wood if required.

Step 2
(209) Apply a liberal coating of tung oil with either a brush (a) or rag (b). Leave the oil to soak into the wood for fifteen to thirty minutes. Wipe off the excess with a clean rag and leave it to dry, preferably overnight. As with linseed oil, the drying time will depend on working conditions. Drying can take as long as two days.

Step 3

(210) Lightly cut back the surface with either flour paper (a) held in your fingers, or with 0000 grade steel wool. Take care not to cut back to the bare wood.

(211) Narrow edges such as those on the frame can be difficult in this respect, and you will find it better to use flour paper wrapped tightly round a glass-paper block for these (a). Keep the block flat and level, and in contact with both edges. Dust off thoroughly and apply a second liberal coat of oil. Leave for a few minutes to soak in, then wipe off the excess with the grain as before and leave to dry.

Step 4

(212) Apply a last coat with 0000 grade steel wool, working with the grain. Leave for a few minutes and buff up with a soft cloth.

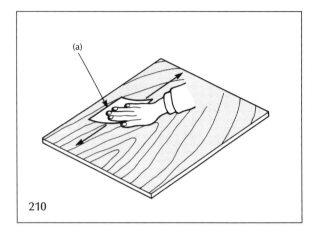

210

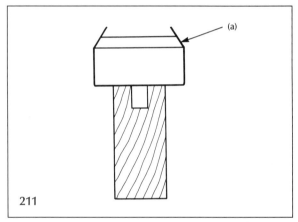

211

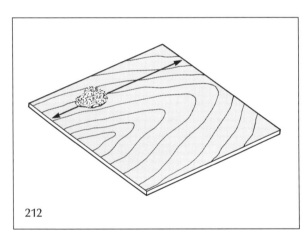

212

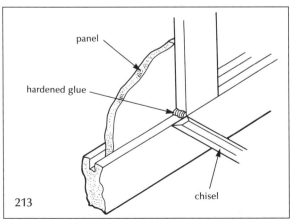

panel

hardened glue

chisel

213

Step 5 (Optional)

If you want a higher sheen than the tung oil produces, you can apply a coat or two of wax polish. Make sure the oil is dry first, two or three days being ideal. Ordinary household furniture paste wax will give a good finish but some waxes will give a higher shine than others. Apply the wax with the grain, using a soft cloth. Leave for a few minutes for the solvents to evaporate and buff up with a clean, soft cloth.

(213) Before gluing the components together, remove the tape masking the gluing area. After gluing, excess glue from the inside corners can either be cleaned off straight away or left to harden. As the glue will not stick to oil or wax, it will lift away easily and cleanly with a chisel. Outside surfaces are finished in the same way. To maintain the finish if you have not waxed, apply a fresh coat of oil occasionally. Leave it for a few minutes, wipe it dry and then buff it up. If you have waxed the surface then apply an occasional coat of wax polish.

Teak Oil Finish

Raw linseed and pure tung oil have no additives. This is not true of teak oil, for which there is no standard of production. The basic ingredient is linseed oil and it may or may not contain tung oil; all will contain drying agents of some kind.

(214) It was developed for finishing teak and teak-veneered furniture. In its natural state, teak is an oily wood and the application of more oil enhances its

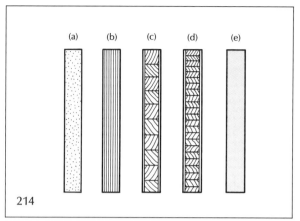

214

natural beauty. Teak oil produces a low lustre and is suitable for use on all hardwoods and all types of veneered manufactured boarding, such as chipboard (a), plywood (b), blockboard (c), laminboard (d) and MDF (e).

(215) To describe this finish, a bookcase with loose shelves is used because it emphasizes some difficulties you may encounter in finishing your own projects.

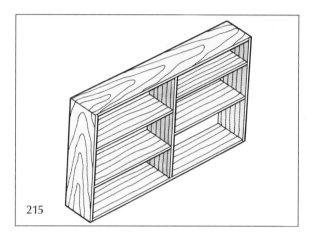

215

(216) For the bookcase shown and similar constructions, it is possible to use teak oil on the inside surfaces after gluing up and achieve a satisfactory finish, taking into account that all of them are either underneath or hidden by books. However, for top-quality work and in situations where these surfaces are seen, they must be treated to the same degree of care and attention as the outside. To achieve this, oiling is best done before

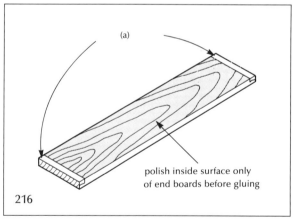

(a)

polish inside surface only
of end boards before gluing

216

assembly. Before the finishing begins, you must mask off (a) areas requiring glue later, as in the previous example.

(217) The main problem you will encounter is that posed by the central partition, which has to be oiled on both sides. The same problem will present itself on the loose shelves. If you work through the polishing routine on each side separately you will double the time needed to apply the finish, although this method can be followed if you wish.

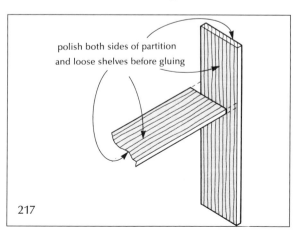

polish both sides of partition
and loose shelves before gluing

217

(218) The alternative is to have ready some large pieces of clean cloth – old sheets or pillowcases cut to the appropriate size are ideal. Place these on the polishing board and, having oiled one side, turn the work over to oil the other side. After oiling both sides, the work can carefully be left so that each side can dry out equally. How this is done will be dependent on your own working situation, but you should consider the problem *before* oiling begins.

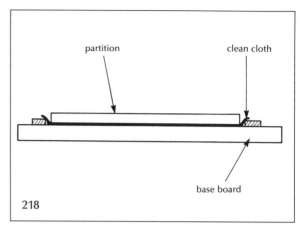

218

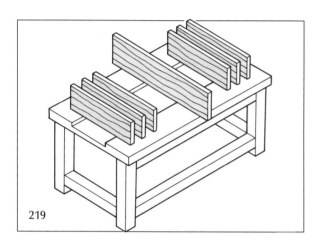

219

(219) If you have a separate work surface which will not be jogged or knocked when subsequent pieces are being oiled, and as long as the back edges have been planed perfectly square ('care with one stage makes the next easier') then the work will stand on those. Leave adequate space between them to allow a good air flow.

(220) If a work surface is not available, then a run of free wall will enable oiled pieces to be leaned separately against it. It will need to be prepared beforehand – sweep the floor and dust off the wall. You could also make up a three-sided box, using pins as support, or screw a batten to the wall with pins or dowels to do a similar job.

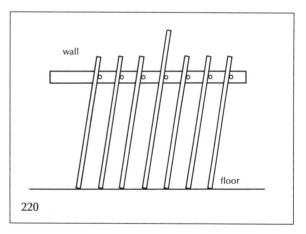

220

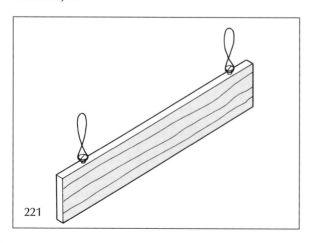

221

(221) If all else fails, two screws at the back edge of each piece, with either wire or string already attached and hung on nails in the wall or ceiling, will suffice. The latter method is not recommended if you are oiling in the lounge, but it does emphasize the need to plan finishing operations. If you do resort to the hanging method, the last thing you want are clouds of dust being knocked off the workshop rafters as you hammer nails into them. The backs of bookcases and cabinets are best oiled flat and applied to the work afterwards, even if you have opted to assemble the rest of the work before oiling.

Finishing Method

Step 1
Fill and stain the wood, if required.

Step 2
(222) Apply a liberal coat of oil with either a brush or rag. Leave to soak in for fifteen minutes and wipe off the surplus with a clean, dry cloth. On larger areas, you will need to change the cloth as each piece becomes wet.

222

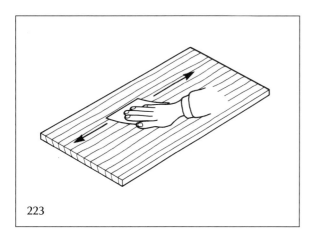

223

Step 3
(223) Use flour paper held in your fingers or 0000 grade steel wool, and cut back lightly until smooth. Remove all dust thoroughly. Apply a second coat and leave to dry.

Step 4
Repeat Step 3.

Step 5
(224) Apply the third coat with a rag. Leave to harden for at least twenty-four hours.

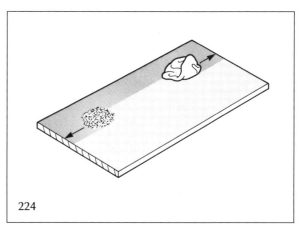

224

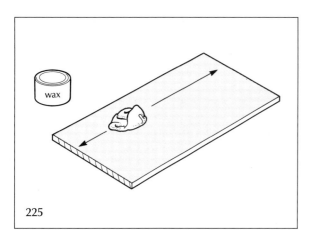

225

Step 6
(225) After cutting back lightly with flour paper, apply the last coat very sparingly with a rag, rubbing vigorously to spread the oil. Buff up with a clean, dry cloth. Wax can be used on top if you wish when the last coat has had time to harden.

Other Types of Oil Finishes

Danish and Scandinavian Oil

These are based on tung oil but will also contain resins and other oils, together with drying agents. The method of finishing is the same as that described for teak oil.

Cedar Oil

This is a linseed-based oil with drying agents added. It can be used as an alternative to boiled linseed oil.

Lemon Oil

This is different from the other oils. It is made from oil produced from lemon grass, to which drying agents are added. It smells very similar to the citrus lemon, but has no other connection with the fruit. It is not as waterproof as the other oils but it can be used on some furniture instead of teak oil or Danish oil. Because of its pleasant smell, it is ideal for use on the inside of a blanket chest where you want to seal the surface but not produce a finish. It is also suitable for the inside of drawers and cupboards. You should ensure that the oil is thoroughly dry before putting the piece into use. Apply the oil with a brush or rag – only one coat is needed to provide a sealed surface, although more coats can be applied if you wish.

Olive Oil

Where food is concerned, it is better to use an oil which contains no chemicals and which will not taint the food. Olive oil should be used on salad bowls, cutting boards and other wooden utensils. As an alternative, you can use any other type of cooking oil but these do tend to remain sticky. Apply the oil sparingly with a clean cloth and rub well into the wood.

Outside Work

Oils give a good finish for outdoor furniture as they do not provide a film on the surface in the same way as varnish does. The lack of a film means that oils do not peel, and this is a definite advantage. It is necessary to re-oil at yearly intervals to maintain the colour of the wood. You can use any of the oils previously described, the only exceptions being lemon oil and olive oil. For outside work, oils are best applied liberally with a brush and left to soak in for a longer period of time than for inside work. Maximum penetration is required to give the best protection against weather. The bottoms of legs on tables and chairs can be left standing in oil for a few hours. Capillary action draws the oil up the grain, sealing the end grain to prevent water creeping upwards.

Oil for Cleaning Furniture

In normal use, exposed surfaces on furniture are dusted and polished regularly. Sometimes a more thorough cleaning job is needed, which will involve removing drawers and emptying bookcases. Internal corners become dirty and very dry. A good cleaner can be made by mixing linseed oil (boiled or raw) with an equal amount of turpentine or white spirit. Heat the oil using the two-pan method, and mix it with the thinners thoroughly. Apply sparingly with a paintbrush, working into the corners and along the grain. Wipe off immediately with a dry cloth. Buff until dry.

GENERAL ADVICE ON OILING

- Embark on the traditional method of oiling only if you are willing to devote plenty of time and energy to the finish.
- When using manufactured oils, use the product of one manufacturer throughout.
- If directions allow for the addition of wood dye to the oil, use the dye from the same manufacturer – it will have been tested for compatibility.

226

SAFETY WITH OILS

- Oils containing drying agents dry by oxidization – they take in oxygen. Rags used for oiling are therefore liable to spontaneous combustion.
- Used rags should be laid out flat to dry or washed in hot, soapy water.
- As an alternative, used rags can be placed in a sealed container for disposal.

227

Wax finishing was known to the ancient Egyptians and is probably the oldest finish known to man. In more recent history all the best known cabinet makers such as Sheraton, Chippendale, Adam and Hepplewhite used wax as a finish. French polish only arrived on the scene after they had died. The usual practice at that time was to rub a piece of cork on a block of beeswax and then transfer the wax from the cork to the work by vigorous and hard rubbing, building up many layers. It is easier to apply the wax as a paste.

(228) Wax finishing is simplicity itself in that it requires little or no skill. Like the basic oil finish, a wax finish on bare wood involves building up a number of layers of polish, although it is generally regarded as a quicker finish. It is not as hard wearing and will be more easily marked by spillages. Wax does not provide such a good seal on the surface and areas around handles of doors and drawers tend to become dirty. Further waxing and subsequent rubbing will only spread the dirt and push it into the wood. This will show up particularly on light woods. You can overcome the problem to a large extent with a finish known as semi-waxing. Because wax is applied in the initial stages with a stiff, shoe-type brush, it is ideal for carved work.

Main Types of Wax

The main types of wax are beeswax, made from the comb of the honey-bee, and carnuba wax, which is a vegetable product and much harder than beeswax. Other types include Japan wax, Ozokerite wax and paraffin wax. Various combinations of these, together with turpentine, are used to make a wide range of ready-made polishes, some of which will contain petrol to make them dry faster. With so many to choose from it is difficult to give advice on what to buy, except to say that polishes containing carnuba wax will give a harder surface and can be buffed to a higher gloss. Waxes made entirely from carnuba are liable to flake if repeated coats are applied, and for this reason it is normally mixed with beeswax.

Making Your Own Wax

It is quite simple to make your own wax: all you need is a block of beeswax and pure turpentine. Use bleached beeswax if you want a light-coloured polish for light woods, or raw beeswax for all other woods.

Coloured waxes, known as stain waxes, have coloured pigments added and are best obtained ready made.

REQUIREMENTS FOR WAX POLISHING

Stain (optional)
Must be spirit or water
Wax – ready made
with high proportion of beeswax
or
Wax – made yourself
Beeswax
Carnuba wax
(optional but makes wax harder and less sticky)
Turpentine
Lighter fuel
(optional but makes the wax dry faster)
Two clean shoe brushes with fairly stiff bristles
Cloth

REQUIREMENTS FOR SEMI-WAX POLISHING

Stain (optional)
Sealer
either
Sanding sealer
or
French polish
(white or transparent for light woods; garnet
or button for dark woods)
or
Varnish
or
Brushing lacquers
Wax
Shoe brushes (optional)
Soft cloth

228

(229) Shred the wax and dissolve it in the turpentine. The process is speeded up if you warm the turpentine using the two-pan system. Add the turpentine until you have a paste which is about the same consistency as soft butter – a stiffer paste is harder to apply. This will give you the basic polish. You can, if you wish, add a little carnuba wax to give a slightly harder surface and a little petrol (cigarette lighter fuel) which will make the wax faster drying. If you use a ready-made wax, select one that has a high percentage of beeswax. Remove wax from the heat before adding turpentine and lighter fuel.

Coloured waxes, known as stain waxes, have coloured pigments added and are best obtained ready made.

Finishing Method for Wax Polish

(230) Wax polishing can be carried out on inside surfaces before assembly if you wish. Although not as important as for oil as less rubbing is required, it will

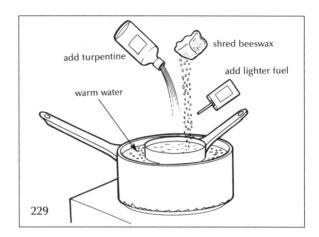

229

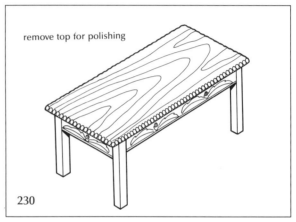

230

still give the best finish on these surfaces. Mask off gluing areas and use a polishing board as described in the previous section (*see* page 66).

Step 1
Grain filler is not normally used for wax polishing as the polish itself tends to fill the grain, but you can use grain filler if you wish. You can stain under wax, but unless you use the semi-wax method do not use an oil-based stain – if you do, the applied wax will dissolve the stain which will be picked up by the brush, resulting in a patchy colour. If you do not want to use the semi-wax method, use either a water or spirit stain.

Step 2
(231) Apply the wax with the brush rubbing it well into the grain. Use a fairly generous amount but be sure to spread it evenly. On flat surfaces, work with the grain, and on carved work use a circular movement **(232)**. This will ensure that the wax is pushed into all the corners.

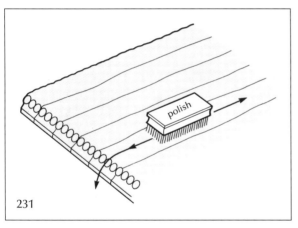

231

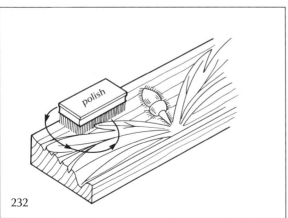

232

After waxing, set the work aside for at least one day. The surface should not be buffed up until all the turpentine has evaporated, and the time this will take depends on your working conditions. If you have added a little petrol to the polish, the drying time will be reduced. Place the polishing brush in a polythene bag to keep it soft.

Step 3
(233) Use a second brush for the buffing up (it is a good idea to mark the brushes if they are identical). You will need plenty of elbow grease, and be sure to pay attention to the corners if you are polishing the work after it has been assembled. Buff with the grain on flat surfaces and with circular movements on carved work (234).

Step 4
After working hard with the brush, finish off with a soft cloth, buffing well to reveal the shine.

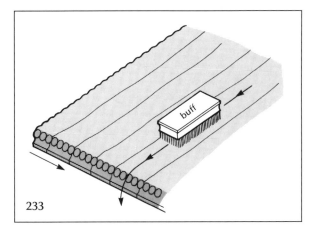

233

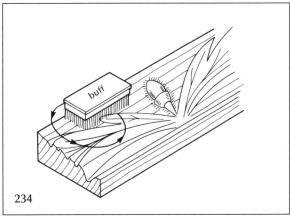

234

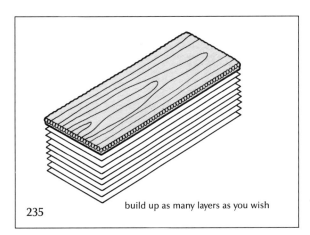

235   build up as many layers as you wish

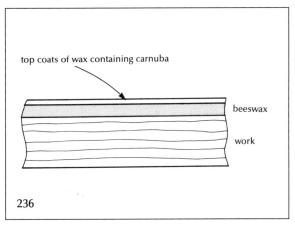

top coats of wax containing carnuba

beeswax

work

236

Step 5
Cut back very lightly with flour paper and dust off.

Step 6 Onwards
Apply subsequent wax coats in the same way as before, using the brush for the first two or three applications. A rag can be used to apply the polish and to buff up other coats, if needed. You can probably dispense with the flour paper as well if you are working in a relatively dust-free situation. Assess the surface after each coat has hardened by running your hand gently over the surface to check for smoothness. If it is just very slightly rough, then use old, worn flour paper very lightly.

(235) You can apply as many coats as you wish to build up the finish you want for a particular piece of work. A higher shine can be obtained by finishing with a coat of wax containing a greater percentage of carnuba (236).

Finishing Method for Semi-Wax Polish

This method of wax polishing will speed up the process considerably because the surface is first sealed with french polish or a shellac sanding sealer. This prevents the wax being absorbed into the wood and a good shine can be achieved with only two or three coats of wax. This system must be used if you have used an oil-based stain to colour the wood. On bare wood, or where you have used water or spirit stain, you could use a clear varnish as a sealer, but this will take longer to dry.

Step 1
Fill and stain the wood, if required.

Step 2
If you are using french polish as a sealer, you can use either white, transparent, button or garnet polish. White and transparent polishes will give a minimum colour change to the surface and can be used on light and dark

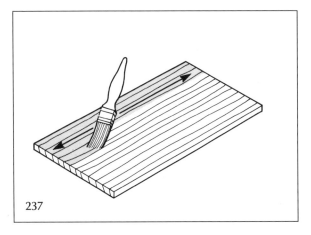

237

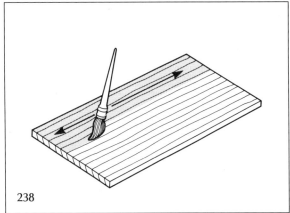

238

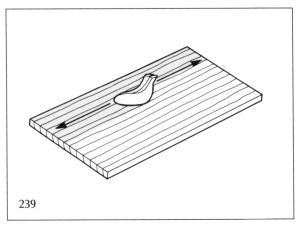

239

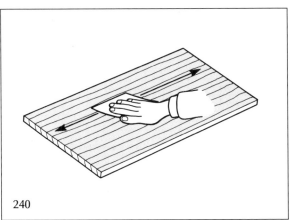

240

woods. Both button and garnet polish will colour the wood slightly. Button polish will give a slight orange tint and garnet more of a brown hue. As in all finishing processes, you should check on a piece of spare wood first. Clear varnish will have the same effect as white or transparent french polish. When used as a sealer, varnish should be thinned with 10 per cent white spirit.

(237) Varnish can be applied with a good quality paintbrush, brushing out well to give a thin coat.

(238) French polish can be used on bare wood and with any stain. It is best applied with a soft polishers' mop, working quickly along the grain. Apply thinly and do not go back to brush it out or the polish will be pulled into a rough surface.

(239) A rubber can also be used to apply french polish, but work in straight strokes with the grain. De-nib between coats (240).

(241) Inside surfaces on work already glued up are best done with a mop as a rubber will not work easily into the corners. Work out from the corners.

Whatever the sealer or method of application you use, leave the first coat to harden. For french polish applied in reasonable conditions, twenty minutes is sufficient. Varnish should be left overnight.

Step 3
Rub down very lightly with flour paper and dust off.

Step 4
(242) If you are working from bare wood without stain, one coat of french polish or varnish is sufficient to seal the surface. If you use an oil stain, apply a second coat of french polish to ensure that the stain is well sealed before applying the wax. It does no harm to give a second coat in all circumstances if you wish. Leave to harden. Lightly rub down with flour paper. Dust off.

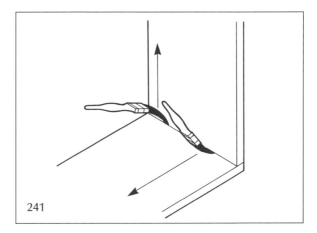

241

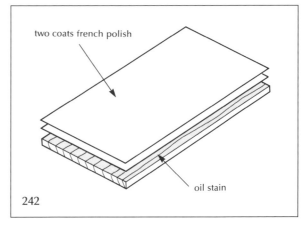

two coats french polish

oil stain

242

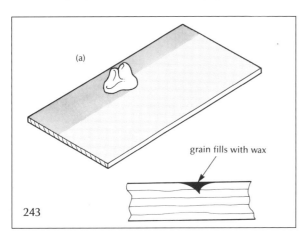

(a)

grain fills with wax

243

Step 5
Having sealed the surface, you can apply as many coats of wax as you like to give the finish you want. Use a shoe-brush or a rag. Give each coat a few minutes for the thinners to evaporate before buffing up.

Coloured Waxes

(243) These are most effective as a stain when used on bare wood, but they can be used at any time in the waxing or semi-waxing process to induce a slightly different tone to the finish (a). Check the result first on a spare piece of wood.

(244) Coloured waxes can be particularly useful in giving an older look to new carvings where the dark waxes can be left a little thicker in the corners (a).

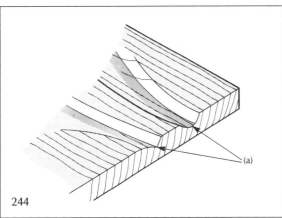

(a)

244

French polishing is generally regarded as a finish which is difficult to do, needing years of continual practice to achieve good results, and one which should, under no circumstances, be tackled by a mere beginner to wood finishing. Much of this attitude has been brought about in the past by people in the trade wishing to keep the mystique of french polishing alive and well.

Good, all-round workers with wood, or cabinet makers, the one-man set-up, have always been pleased to pass on their knowledge and skill to those who have shown interest. In the past it has, in the main, been those workers in the larger institutions employing a great many people who jealously guarded their knowledge and method of working. This was quite simply because they commanded a higher wage than some other workers and obviously made every endeavour to keep their differential. It was also true that a good polisher could make inferior workmanship and materials look good, and so they were extremely valuable to their employers.

None of this should detract from the art and skill of the polisher. The whole polishing process in its entirety does take a long time to learn and master. However, very good results can be achieved with a little practice, and the sense of achievement at having mastered a new skill is an end in itself, not to mention the versatility that french polishing offers as a finish to enhance your work.

When it was first introduced into Britain from France in about 1820, many regarded french polish as an inferior finish to the wax and linseed oil used previously. It was viewed in much the same way as traditionalists regard new materials today. It is worth noting that the most well known and highly regarded British furniture makers all lived and produced their work before the introduction of french polish.

Since the introduction of french polishing, much has been written on the subject. Very old books can mislead the beginner into thinking that a vast range of materials are needed. Some descriptions talk about obtaining ox-gall from any butcher's slaughterman at 6d. a gill, which should then be filtered through crushed bone charcoal before using. Having been strained, the resultant liquid will last the polisher until it 'turns bad'. Half a pound of lamp-black is also difficult to obtain these days!

Far from being complicated some applications to which ready-made polishes can be put are simplicity itself,

HISTORY OF FURNITURE FINISHES

Wax

Age of oak – up to the end of the 17th century

Wax and Linseed

Age of Walnut – 1660 to 1733
Age of mahogany – 1733 onwards
1820 – introduction of french polishing
Thomas Chippendale 1718–1779
Robert Adam 1760–1792
George Hepplewhite 1760–1790
Thomas Sheraton 1790–1806
These famous furniture makers all lived and produced their work before french polish was introduced into Britain

Materials Required

Polish – French, button, garnet, white or transparent
Polishing mop
Cotton cloth
Wadding or unmedicated cotton wool
Methylated spirit
Linseed oil or white oil
Clean, dry screw-top glass jar
Grade 0000 steel wool (optional)
Pumice powder or rottenstone (optional)

245

although it would be wrong to describe those methods as french polishing.

Polish can be sprayed on using a small air-brush which can be very useful for restoration work and furniture repairs which require small areas of new wood to be coloured in with the rest of the work. This coloured polish can be made up, as described on page 88, and, with a little practice, it can be used to very good effect. A polishing rubber is used to even out any spray marks and to blend the new area into the original finish surrounding it. This method is not intended to replace traditional techniques but rather to be used in conjunction with them.

FRENCH POLISHING

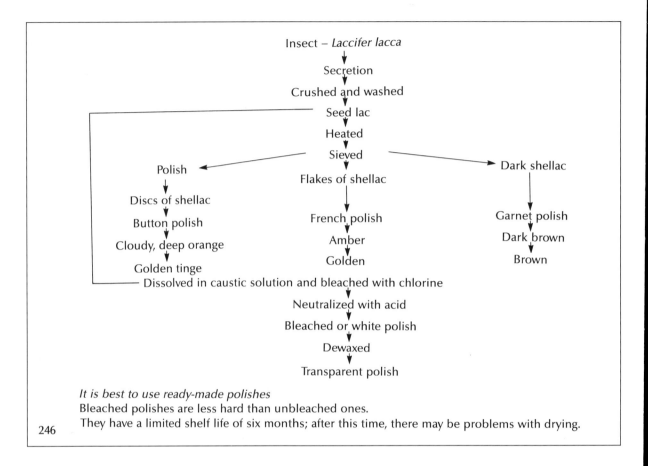

Insect – *Laccifer lacca*
↓
Secretion
↓
Crushed and washed
↓
Seed lac
↓
Heated
↓
Sieved
↓
Flakes of shellac

Polish ← → Dark shellac

Discs of shellac

Button polish

Cloudy, deep orange

Golden tinge

French polish
↓
Amber
↓
Golden

Garnet polish
↓
Dark brown

Brown

Dissolved in caustic solution and bleached with chlorine
↓
Neutralized with acid
↓
Bleached or white polish
↓
Dewaxed
↓
Transparent polish

It is best to use ready-made polishes
Bleached polishes are less hard than unbleached ones.
They have a limited shelf life of six months; after this time, there may be problems with drying.

246

Compared with linseed oil and the more modern finishes such as cellulose, acid lacquers and polyurethanes, it is not family-proof, but it does give a wonderful finish to wood which enhances its natural beauty. French polishes are now available which have additives to make it more resistant to heat, water and alcohol, but they are generally more difficult to use and should be avoided to begin with.

Basic french polish is made from shellac which is dissolved in industrial alcohol. Shellac is an organic substance derived from an insect – *Laccifer lacca* – which flourishes in India and other far-eastern countries. The insect feeds on the young shoots of trees and forms a secretion which covers the swarm and then hardens. This is collected, crushed, washed and separated from the twigs, and when dry it is known as Seed Lac. This is then heated to make it molten and pushed through a sieve. The purest shellac is pushed through first and dropped on to a cold surface where it

spreads out and cools to form a thin disc. The less pure material which follows is stretched into thin sheets and allowed to harden. This is then crushed and made into flakes. Dissolving the discs in industrial alcohol makes button polish; dissolving the flakes in alcohol makes French polish.

To avoid confusion, it should be made clear here that French polish with a capital 'F' refers to the actual polish described above, but when used with a lower case 'f' it refers to all polishes made from shellac and alcohol.

In addition to the French polish and button polish, there is garnet polish which is made from a darker type of shellac.

The polishing process itself consists of applying many thin coats of the chosen polish, the colour of it determining the final colour of the finished piece.

Button polish is a cloudy, deep orange colour and will tend to introduce a golden tinge to the work. French polish is an amber colour and can be used instead of button polish to give a slightly different tinge. Garnet polish is dark brown and therefore will tone down and darken the work – for example, you could use it to darken a very red piece of mahogany. In choosing your polish, you must also bear in mind the colour of the stain if you have used one. The polish can, to some degree, correct a stain that is slightly the wrong shade. If, for example, you feel that the overall effect is too golden, it would be a mistake to use button polish – garnet would be a better choice. These changes of colour induced by the polishing material are fairly small compared with the initial staining, so it is still important to be as accurate as possible with the choice of stain colour, but it does seek to emphasize once again the importance of working a sampler first to check your method.

If you want light woods to remain light, none of the polishes described so far is suitable. You should use either white or transparent polish. This is made commercially by dissolving Seed Lac in a hot, caustic solution of water and then bleaching it with chlorine. Acid is then used as a neutralizing agent. This makes bleached or white polish which will cause very little colour change to the natural colour of the wood.

All shellac contains a very small amount of wax from the insect. If this is removed from the polish by washing it with a petroleum solvent, the result is a polish that will change the colour of the wood by the bare minimum. This is known as transparent polish and is used where paleness is essential.

As seen in previous sections, french polish can also be used to seal an oil stain before varnishing or waxing, and is used as a sealer on bare wood. The one or two coats used for this operation do not impart any great colour change to dark woods, but white or transparent polish should be used on light wood or where no colour change is required at all.

French polish is the most versatile of all the finishes. Not only can the colour be adjusted by the type of polish used, but the separate stage of colouring in the polishing process itself can be used to adjust the final colour, as well. This is described in the section on polishing method (*see* pages 87–9).

Most people are of the opinion that a french-polished finish has to be a high-gloss or mirror-like surface. This is far from the truth. You can stop the polishing at any stage, and with the use of fine matting compounds you can achieve anything, from almost matt to satin lustres and, of course, the piano finish which is normally associated with it.

A very nice finish can be obtained by applying three or four coats of french polish put on with a mop. The procedure is a simple one and can be completed in one day. Allow each coat to harden thoroughly, de-nibbing between each with flour paper. After the final coat has hardened cut back the surface with 0000 grade steel wool and wax to give an open grain finish with a pleasant lustre. It is identical in appearance to satin varnish (*see* page 59) but does not have the same durability. Any of the french polishes can be used depending on colour.

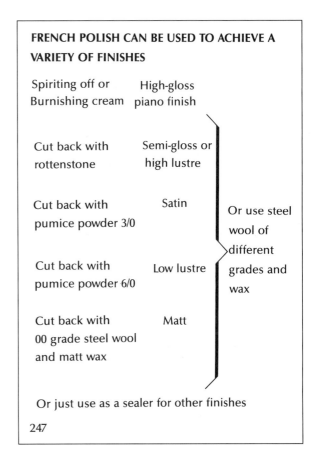

FRENCH POLISH CAN BE USED TO ACHIEVE A VARIETY OF FINISHES

Spiriting off or Burnishing cream	High-gloss piano finish
Cut back with rottenstone	Semi-gloss or high lustre
Cut back with pumice powder 3/0	Satin
Cut back with pumice powder 6/0	Low lustre
Cut back with 00 grade steel wool and matt wax	Matt

Or use steel wool of different grades and wax

Or just use as a sealer for other finishes

247

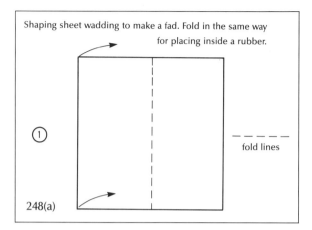

Shaping sheet wadding to make a fad. Fold in the same way for placing inside a rubber.

①

fold lines

248(a)

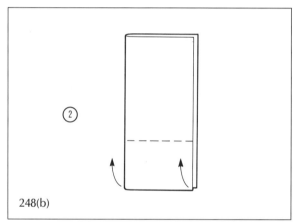

②

248(b)

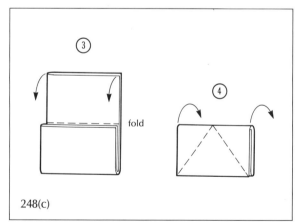

③

fold

④

248(c)

If you are attempting to french polish for the first time, I advise you to use one of the five basic polishes rather than one of the fortified varieties (of which there are many). It is best to buy polish ready made as it is of consistent quality, although it is possible to buy the ingredients if you wish to make your own.

Working Conditions

With other finishes – varnishing, oiling or waxing – the temperature of the workshop is not too important. The only adverse effect on the process is the one of time taken for each coat to harden, but the quality of the work will not be impaired by a cold situation. For french polishing, the temperature must be at least 18°C (65°F), preferably constant and free from draught. Any liquid that evaporates quickly will take heat from the surface to which it is applied. Methylated spirit evaporates very quickly and coats are built up in quick succession. There must be sufficient heat in the room to replace heat loss quickly. Polishing in cold, damp conditions will cause a milky or cloudy appearance, and as soon as this problem is realized, it should be corrected by placing the work in a warm room near a heater until the cloudiness has disappeared. It is also extremely important to have good light to enable you to see the surface you are creating. The light should be in front of you and, by lowering your head, you will see the path being traced out by the rubber. A window in front of the work is ideal.

One of the major causes of a poor finish is dust and dirt and you should give some thought to the problem some time before work commences. It is of little use to sweep off the top of the bench and expect to begin polishing

straight away. It is better to prepare the area the evening before and allow the dust to settle overnight. Use a vacuum cleaner. Some dust is made in rubbing down during the polishing process itself. It is therefore not a good idea to heat the area with a fan heater as this will only circulate the dust and make the problem worse.

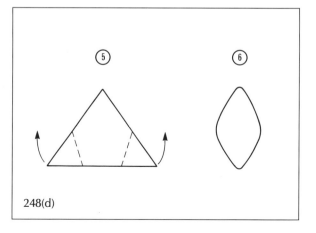

⑤

⑥

248(d)

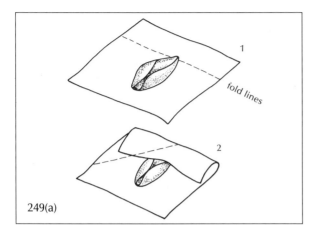

1

fold lines

2

249(a)

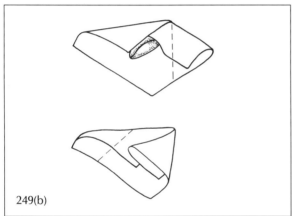

249(b)

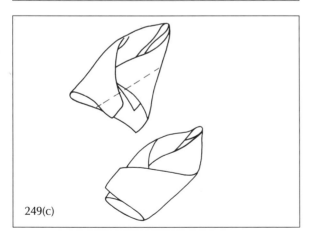

249(c)

The Polishing Rubber

The main tool of the polisher is the rubber. It is made by wrapping a piece of wadding inside a square of cotton. The best rubbers are made from the best materials – you can use a piece of old shirt, but you will find that it will wear into a hole far more quickly than a piece of new 100 per cent cotton bought for the purpose. Cotton wool can be substituted for polishers' wadding, but it will tend to form a soggy lump and will not be as manageable as wadding. It takes a lot of polish to charge a newly made rubber, so you want it to last as long as possible. Used rubbers are easier to use than new ones.

(248) Some wadding is sold in sheet form and must be folded as shown before it is placed on to the cotton. A piece of wadding 230–250mm (9–10in) square gives an average sized rubber. Use the same size square of cotton.

(249) If the wadding is in the form of a cylindrical block, tear off a lump which will fill the area of your outstretched hand – about 50mm (2in) thick. Make this into a rough pear shape before placing it on to the cotton. You will soon find by trial and error how much wadding to use to make various sizes of rubber. They can be made to suit the work in hand – for example, small rubbers can be more easily pointed for polishing into corners, and a large table top will demand a larger rubber than a stool top. Place the wadding on the cotton square and fold it over to give the shape shown.

Before charging the rubber, you will need a screw-top glass jar in which to store it between polishing stages. A drop of linseed oil on the thread of the jar will prevent the lid from sticking. Rubbers stored in this way will

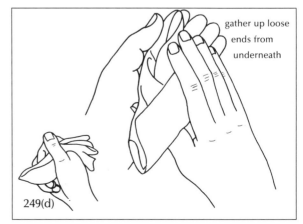

gather up loose ends from underneath

249(d)

keep soft for many months. If you are using different polishes, i.e. button polish and garnet, you will need a rubber for each. Rubbers made for the colouring stage can also be stored to use again.

(250) Not all polishers advise the same technique for charging the rubber. Some advocate dipping the rubber into a shallow container of polish until it is saturated. The rubber is then pressed on to a clean, spare piece of wood, cardboard or the back of a piece of glass-paper. This removes surplus polish and distributes the polish evenly throughout the rubber. Throughout the polishing process, it is imperative that the polish and the face of the rubber are kept dust-free. Having a large surface area of clean polish open on the bench increases the possibility of dust contaminating it. Similarly, pressing the rubber on an exposed surface increases the chance of dust being transferred to the work, but it does have the advantage of not disturbing the shape of the rubber.

(251) Another method is to store the polish in a glass bottle with either a very narrow neck or one that will restrict the flow of polish when tipped up (a vinegar bottle is ideal). This will keep the polish clean through-out the working period. The rubber is charged by opening it out and pouring a limited amount of polish into the middle of the wadding. Press it firmly into the palm of your other hand until you can see a small amount of polish at the edges of the rubber. This will distribute the polish evenly **(252)**. As well as picking up less dust, it is also less wasteful.

Try each method and adopt the one that suits you best. Incidentally, it is not a good idea to keep the polish on the far side of, or in front of the work – if you reach over the work to recharge your rubber, there is a danger that your cuffs may rub on the soft polish you have just applied. Never charge the rubber over the top of the work; keep the polish and your position for charging the rubber away from the work.

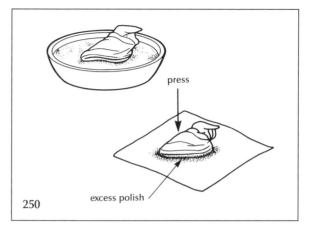

press

excess polish

250

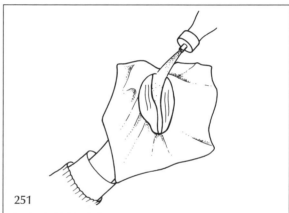

251

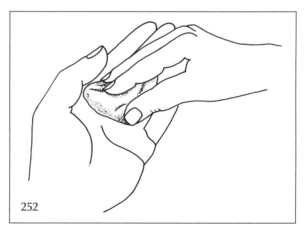

252

(253) Shows the method of holding the rubber whilst polishing.

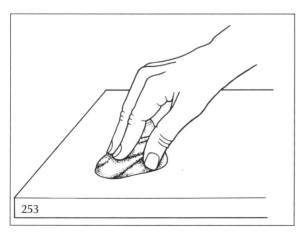

253

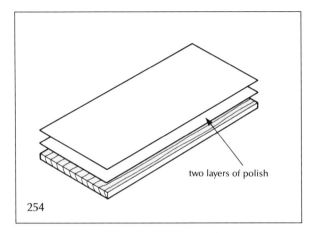

two layers of polish

254

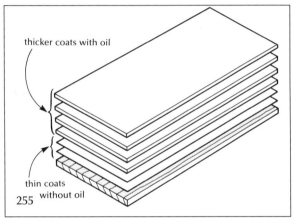

thicker coats with oil

thin coats
without oil

255

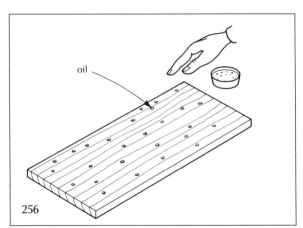

oil

256

(257) Alternatively, use your fingertip to transfer the oil directly to the rubber, or use the thumb which is holding the rubber. A dropper can also be used. Whichever method you prefer, use only the tiniest amount to keep the rubber travelling smoothly across the work.

The Use of Oil

Oil is used on the face of the rubber to lubricate it and to prevent it dragging across the soft polish, causing it to 'pull up'. Use only raw linseed or white mineral oil for this purpose. The amount you use is critical, and it should not be used at all until the wood has been sealed with a couple of layers of polish.

(254) If you are using the process of applying french polish with a rubber just to apply a seal to the surface for taking other finishes, then do not use any. Instead, build up a few thinner coats of polish by going over the surface a couple of times, and then leaving it to harden for twenty minutes. De-nib with flour paper and work the surface again a couple of times only. This process can be repeated if you wish to create a heavier base for wax polishing.

(255) Indeed, by using the above method, it is possible to do the entire job of french polishing without using any oil at all, but the length of time is increased because only thin layers can be applied before the surface becomes sticky. Oil therefore allows the rubber to be used for a longer period of time. Some polishers are of the opinion that using oil gives a tougher, more durable and less brittle finish than one produced without, and I do not disagree with this view.

(256) As in charging the rubber, there are different methods of applying the oil to the face of the rubber. One is to dip your fingertip in the oil and sprinkle it very sparingly on the work where it will be picked up by the rubber.

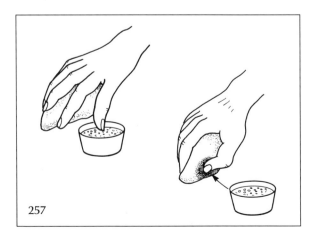

257

Polishing Method

(258) Every polisher has a slightly different way of working, each having found his or her own method suitable for producing consistently good work. The method described here is just one of them and, with a little practice, it will give you good results. I advise you not to start on a valuable piece of furniture or one that has been a long time in the making. Some time spent working on samplers and familiarizing yourself with the rubber will be time well spent.

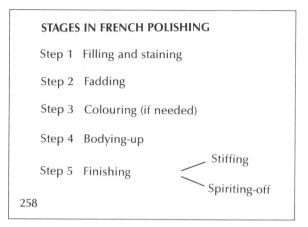

STAGES IN FRENCH POLISHING

Step 1   Filling and staining

Step 2   Fadding

Step 3   Colouring (if needed)

Step 4   Bodying-up

Step 5   Finishing

    Stiffing

    Spiriting-off

258

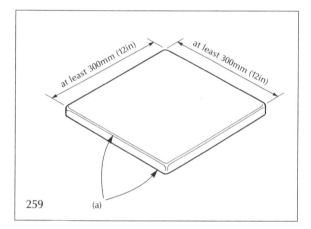

259   (a)

at least 300mm (12in)
at least 300mm (12in)

(259) Off-cuts of good-quality veneered manufactured boarding are ideal for samplers since they do not take too long to prepare. They should be a reasonable size, not less than 300mm (12in) square, and preferably a little larger. Prepare at least four, although half a dozen would be better so that they can be worked in succession. Round off the corners and edges well (a) to avoid snagging the rubber face and tearing the cotton.

(260) Preparation should be thorough: assuming that you will be working through to the spiriting-off stage, remember that any blemishes will show very clearly under a mirror finish. Flour paper will give a sufficiently good surface if used thoroughly.

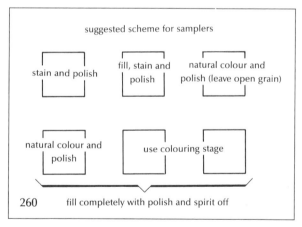

suggested scheme for samplers

stain and polish   fill, stain and polish   natural colour and polish (leave open grain)

natural colour and polish   use colouring stage

260   fill completely with polish and spirit off

(261) The boards must be fixed securely to the bench, using either a polishing board, or G-cramps and strips of wood as spacing blocks (a). These should be thinner than the samplers themselves.

Step 1: Filling and Staining

Fill and stain, if required. The best polishing does not use grain filler, but instead uses the polish to fill the grain (as described on page 46).

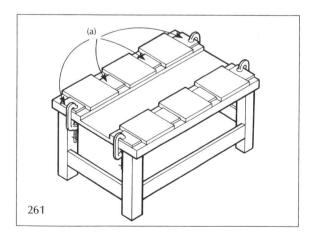

261   (a)

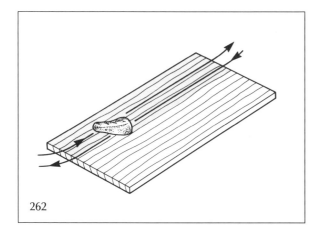

262

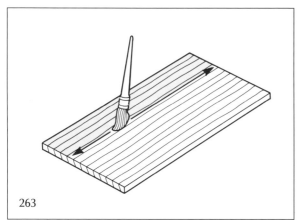

263

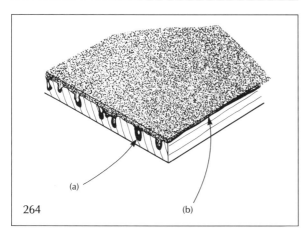

(a)

264 (b)

Repeat the process four of five times, by which time there should be a good layer of polish on the surface and the fadding is complete.

Step 2: Fadding

Fadding could be called heavy bodying-up since it is the initial application of polish which seals the surface and gives a good body of polish on which the subsequent finish is built up. *No oil is used in fadding.* The polish can be applied with a fad or with a polishers' mop or a rubber. A fad is simply a piece of wadding shaped as shown previously, soaked in polish and allowed to dry. This is prepared the previous day. At the time the polishing commences, it is softened with methylated spirit, the surplus being squeezed out. The fad is allowed to harden with polish first to bind the wadding together and to prevent loose threads being deposited on the surface.

(262) Charge the fad with polish. Work along the grain from top to bottom. Try to glide it on to the surface and off again at the far end. The mop is used in the same way **(263)**.

(264) Avoid dragging against the corner at the beginning of the stroke as this will cause a nasty run of polish at the edge (a). Avoid squeezing polish over the edges (b) which can also leave marks.

(265) Overlap each stroke slightly. You need sufficient pressure on the fad to leave a fairly thick film of polish on the surface, without leaving long pools of wet polish (a). An overloaded mop can cause the same problem. Increase the pressure as the fad dries out. Recharge as necessary. Leave the sampler to dry. If you are working six samplers, the first will be dry by the time you have finished the last one. Use a piece of flour paper and go over the whole surface, just enough to make it smooth. Clean it off using the palm of your hand.

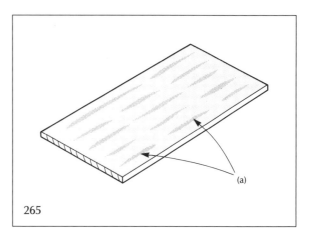

(a)

265

(266) The alternative method for applying the polish uses a polishers' mop. A paintbrush is not suitable as the bristles are too coarse. Mops are available in different sizes and have very fine hairs rather than bristles. They are made of either bear, zarino or squirrel hair, and there are also artificial substitutes for these. They are fairly expensive, but are essential for the brushing method. A size 10 mop will do most jobs. If you are finishing the inside of work which has already been glued up, the mop method is best. Work outwards from the corner along the grain.

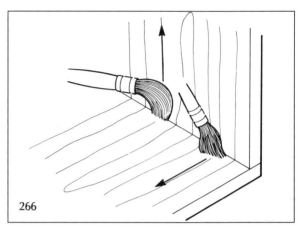

266

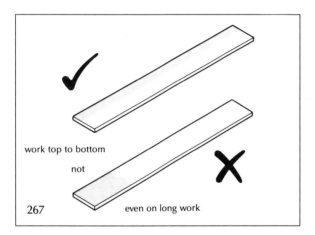

work top to bottom

not

267   even on long work

(267) Apply the polish evenly with a mop which is fairly wet, but not wet enough to leave long, wet pools of polish. On large areas, work a complete length of grain from top to bottom. Avoid working narrow areas and then joining on. Work the mop off edges to avoid runs on these surfaces. Leave to dry before using flour paper as with the fad. Repeat the process four or five times.

(268) For carved work, a brush must be used to avoid filling lower areas with polish (a). Use a fairly dry brush to keep the carving crisp, and apply extra coats if needed.

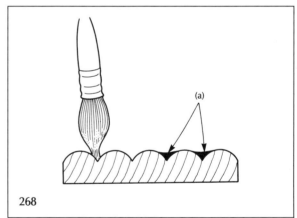

(a)

268

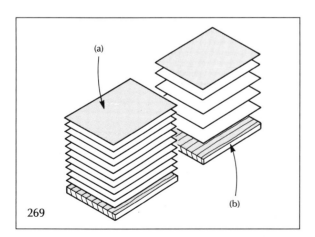

(a)

(b)

269

(269) If you are using a rubber, it is best to make a new one. It can be used later for bodying-up. Do not use one that has previously been used for bodying-up as it is likely to have traces of oil on the face. Use the rubber in the same way as for the fad, with long strokes from end to end and working from top to bottom. Use light pressure to begin with, increasing this as it dries. Re-charge as necessary. Leave to dry and de-nib, then repeat the process four or five times. More coats are needed with a rubber (a) than with a fad or mop (b).

Step 3: Colouring

Colouring is probably the stage where you will see that french polishing is the most versatile of all hand finishes. It allows you to obtain exactly the right colour, shade or tone you want.

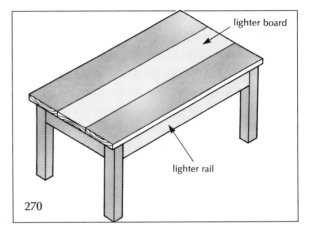

lighter board

lighter rail

270

(270) On new work it can be used to tone in areas that are lighter. The same species of wood can vary in shade considerably, not only from tree to tree, but also in different areas of the same plank. A table top with several boards across its width can show a marked difference in colour from board to board. General staining all over with the same stain will simply darken each board by an equal amount, and lighter areas will, therefore, remain lighter even though the colour has been changed. This may give the desired effect, but if not, it can sometimes be corrected at the staining stage by mixing a darker shade for these areas. The same would apply to a rail which was lighter than the rest of the piece. Colouring during french polishing is another alternative and, if necessary, can be used to make final adjustments. It can also be used to change the overall colour slightly to make an exact match with any existing furniture.

new back leg

271

(271) For restoration and repair work it is invaluable, especially when a complete new piece has been made which must match the rest of the work, or where a new patch of veneer is laid and coloured in with a pencil brush **(272)**.

(273) A good example of where colouring would be used can be illustrated by discussing the restoration of a mahogany extending table. With our table, the loose centre board has been lost some time in the past; loose boards are stored separately from the table. During a

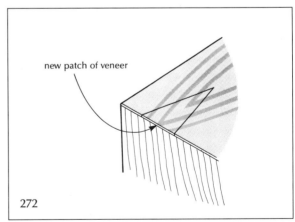

new patch of veneer

272

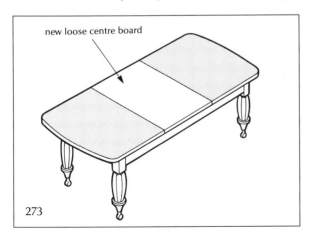

new loose centre board

273

period in its history, it was placed in a sunny position and the colour of the top mellowed from a deep red mahogany to a light brown, golden colour. The new leaf, also made of mahogany, is far too red and dark to match the existing top.

One way is to bleach the new board and stain it to match, as near as possible, the final colour, leaving any final adjustments for the polishing process. Assuming that all our attempts to bleach this particular board fail, there is now no alternative but to take away the redness by polishing. This is done by applying a light yellowish-green polish in very thin coats until the redness of the wood seen through the translucent coloured polish gives the desired effect. After colouring, garnet polish is used to body-up, just to tone down the colour a little.

(274) Colouring is produced with a mixture of spirit-soluble analine dye powder, methylated spirit and polish. It is important to make a very weak colour so that each layer makes an almost imperceptible change to the work. The colour change is brought about by the application of several very thin coats applied with a rubber. It is better to have the colour a little too weak than too strong. In practice, this will mean that more coats are needed to achieve the same colour change as would be brought about by a stronger mix, but the change is more manageable.

(275) As a rough guide for mixing, you will need a 6mm (¼in) piece of wood to use as a measure. Use as much powder as will stay on the end for 6mm (¼in) of its length; this will colour 150ml (5fl oz) of polish.

(276) Place the powder in a bottle, add 75ml (2½fl oz) of spirit and shake well. Add 75ml (2½fl oz) of polish and shake well again. If you are using more than one colour (say, yellow and green to make a light green), the total dye powder should equal the quantity given. Mix the lighter colour with the spirit first and then add the darker one to it, a couple of grains at a time – some colours are very potent. Experience plays a great part in

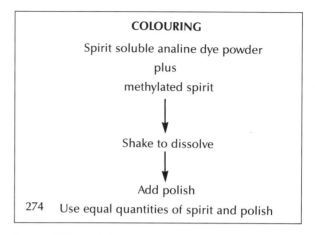

COLOURING

Spirit soluble analine dye powder

plus

methylated spirit

↓

Shake to dissolve

↓

Add polish

274   Use equal quantities of spirit and polish

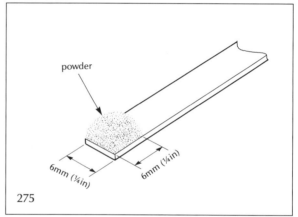

powder

6mm (¼in)

6mm (¼in)

275

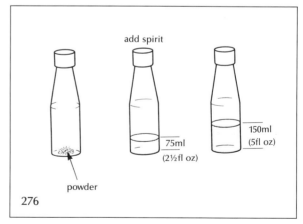

add spirit

75ml
(2½fl oz)

150ml
(5fl oz)

powder

276

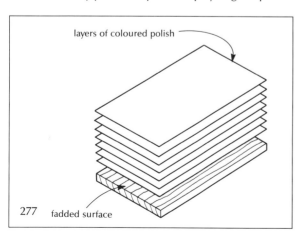

layers of coloured polish

277   fadded surface

colouring, not least in deciding which colour to make up. As with mixing spirit stains, the basics of mixing water colours for painting pictures apply. Resort to paper and a box of paint if it helps but remember the colour of the polish itself will be an ingredient as well when polishing.

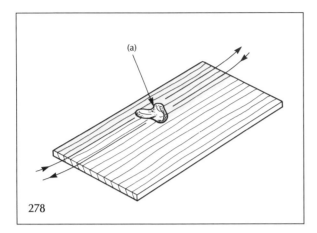

278

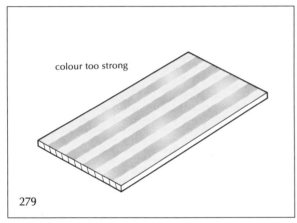

colour too strong

279

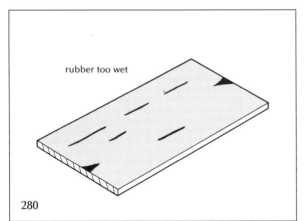

rubber too wet

280

If you intend to leave the grain as open as possible but realise after a fad of polish that you will need to colour then reduce the number of times you go over the surface at that stage. This leaves room for new layers of polish on top of the colouring but still gives the openness you require.

Colouring Method

(278) Colouring is done with a rubber, a new one being made for the purpose (a). When charging the rubber with coloured polish, it should not be too wet otherwise long pools of polish will appear along the edges of the path it traces, and a streaky surface will result. Work with the grain and from top to bottom. As the polish has been diluted with spirit, evaporation will be rapid and, depending on the size of the surface being worked, you can apply several coats in quick succession. It is better not to use oil in this process, and instead you should stop work at the least hint of pulling on the rubber. Leave to dry for a few minutes before continuing.

(279) Whether you colour one or two of the samplers is a matter of choice, but try out the process first before attempting to use it on a piece of furniture. All colouring is a matter of trial and error, and the need for checking on spare wood first cannot be over-stressed. It is also best to check the colour in daylight.

Step 4: Bodying-Up

(281) Bodying-up is the process of building up the main body or thickness of polish. If you have used the colouring stage, then a sufficient thickness of polish must be applied to protect the coloured layer underneath. This is particularly important if the surface is likely to be subjected to a lot of wear – for example, the arms of carver chairs and the tops of chair backs. A good thickness of polish is also crucial if you are intending to cut back the surface later with any of the mild abrasives in order to produce a satin or lustre finish. If you have not used the colouring stage, bodying-up can be stopped at any time to allow openness of grain, or can be continued for a full finish.

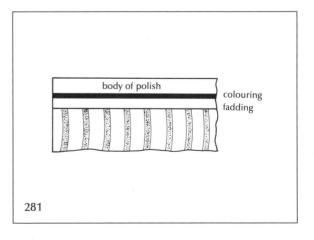

body of polish

colouring fadding

281

Step 4a

The aim of bodying-up is to use the polishing rubber to distribute very thin layers of polish evenly over the surface. You can achieve a finish using the rubber in straight strokes only, but a better distribution of polish is obtained if the rubber is used in several different ways.

(282) Working on the first sampler, begin by using circles. Charge the rubber with polish, then press it in the palm of your other hand to distribute the polish evenly throughout. Use fairly small circles evenly all over the surface, working in rows from top to bottom. The size of the circles will depend on the size of the rubber which, in turn, is relative to the surface being polished. For the size of rubber suggested earlier (*see* page 81) and the samplers, circles of about 50–60mm (2–2½in) in diameter would be ideal, although this is not critical. Each row of circles should just overlap the previous one. Use light pressure to begin with, gradually increasing the pressure as the polish is used up and the rubber becomes drier. Recharge as necessary. Never allow the rubber to stop on the surface, or the polish previously applied will be softened and a mark will be left as the rubber is lifted off. Glide the rubber on to the surface at the start and off again at the end. Go back to the beginning and repeat the circles **(283)**. Then work the other samplers in the same way.

(284) Having finished the last sampler, you can go straight back to the first one and repeat the circles procedure again so that four coats are applied.

(285) Having reached the bottom for the second time on the first sampler, go straight back to the top and run

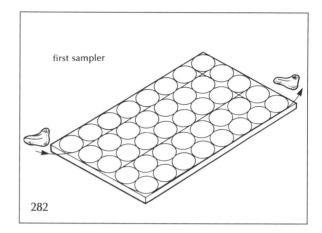

first sampler

282

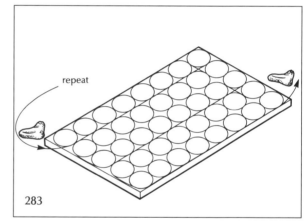

repeat

283

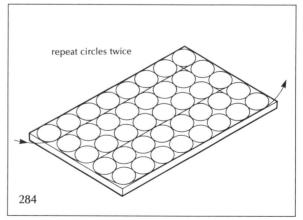

repeat circles twice

284

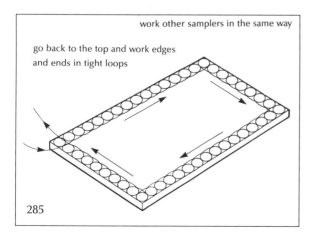

work other samplers in the same way

go back to the top and work edges
and ends in tight loops

285

once round the edges using smaller circles. This will overcome the problem that everyone has, which is the tendency to miss out corners and edges. Work the other samplers in the same way.

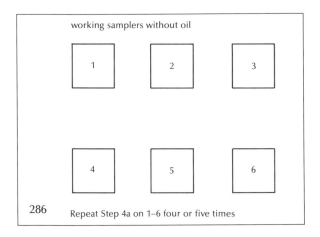

working samplers without oil

1	2	3
4	5	6

286   Repeat Step 4a on 1–6 four or five times

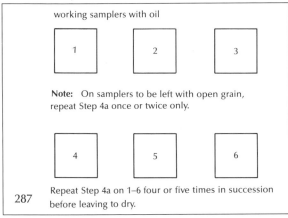

working samplers with oil

1	2	3

Note: On samplers to be left with open grain, repeat Step 4a once or twice only.

4	5	6

287   Repeat Step 4a on 1–6 four or five times in succession before leaving to dry.

(286) If you are polishing without oil, leave the samplers to harden for twenty minutes before continuing.

(287) Using oil on the rubber the whole process can be repeated several times, but at some stage you will find that the rubber begins to pull excessively. There should always be a little resistance to the movement of the rubber as this is a sure sign that it is doing its job, which is to pull the polish along and deposit it evenly on the surface. When the pull becomes excessive, however, the surface of the soft polish will become roughened. As soon as the extra pull is realized, add a tiny quantity of oil as described earlier. When polishing is restarted, there will be a light smear on the surface following the rubber. If you have used too much oil, there will be no resistance to the movement of the rubber at all, and you will see a lot of smearing. As much of the polishing process is governed by vision, good light is essential. Your head should be low, sighting the work across the surface, and it should also bob around quite a bit to establish the best view. Sense of touch through the rubber is equally important. This is difficult to describe, but you can obtain a good indication of the correct feel by experimenting with a piece of glass or a mirror.

(288) Polish the glass with a dry duster to make sure it is clean and lay it flat on the bench. Place the heel of your polishing hand on it and make circular movements. Increase the pressure until you feel some resistance between hand and glass. This is how the rubber should feel when it has just a spot of oil on it.

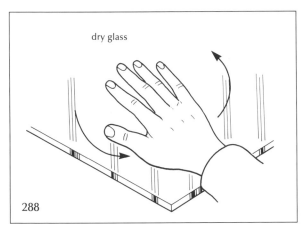

dry glass

288

(289) As a comparison, wet the glass with water and try the same movement. You will feel no resistance and this is the equivalent of using too much oil.

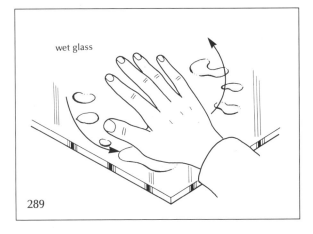

wet glass

289

As the oil is on the rag and not on the wadding, the situation of too much oil is easily rectified by replacing the rag with a new piece wrapped round the existing wadding. The rag will also need replacing when it begins to wear through. Loose strands of cotton underneath the face of the rubber will cause marks. You can move the wadding to a new area of cotton a couple of times before replacement becomes vital. The method of folding the rag when making the rubber, and the subsequent way of holding it ensures that no loose threads from the edges are able to stray underneath.

Step 4b

You will reach a stage where even with the use of oil the surface is sticky and polishing must stop to allow it time to harden off; it is best left overnight. Before polishing begins again, use flour paper held in your fingers. Work over the surface with the grain until it is smooth, and then dust off. If, at any time in the bodying-up, the surface becomes contaminated with dust or debris of

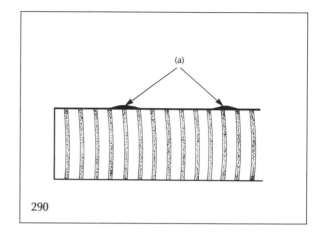

290

any kind, it should be left to harden and papered back before polishing again. It is a mistake to bury dirt in the polish.

(290) Continuing with circles for the complete bodying-up process would not give a level surface, because the circles tend to be the same size and, as the position of the circles on the first row is determined by the edge of the work, the overlap is always in the same place. This causes a build-up of polish in certain places where the circles overlap (a), and it is for this reason that the path of the rubber is changed.

(291)(292)(293) Three different patterns are shown in the diagrams. Which shape you choose is unimportant and you could even use all three in succession. The only criterion is to ensure an even distribution of polish over the entire surface. For the purpose of the samplers, try each and decide which suits you best.

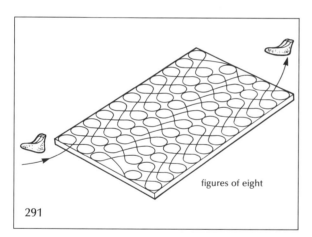

figures of eight

291

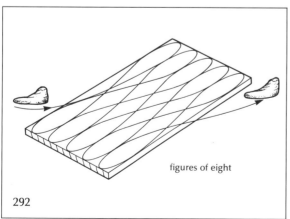

figures of eight

292

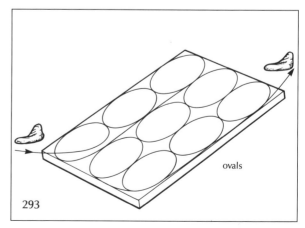

ovals

293

Work on the first sampler and go over it twice before moving on to the next one – this can also be covered four or five times as before. If you intend to keep one or two samplers with open grain, repeat only once or twice on those.

(294) Watch the corners and edges closely. A sign that they are being missed is fullness of grain.

(295) The depth of grain left to fill at the edges should be equal to that in the middle of the work. Go over these areas using tight loops to keep the grain-fill equal if necessary. This is just as important if you intend to keep an open grain. Leave to harden.

How long you spend on each of the bodying-up stages and, therefore, the number of coats you apply will depend on circumstances and is a matter of judgement. If you are aiming for full grain, repeat this stage until the grain is full. Remember that polish sinks on drying and

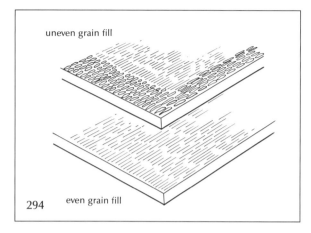

uneven grain fill

even grain fill

294

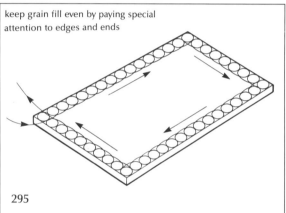

keep grain fill even by paying special attention to edges and ends

295

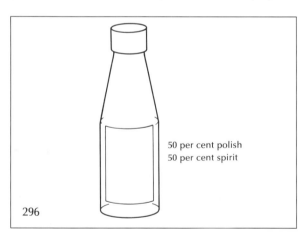

50 per cent polish
50 per cent spirit

296

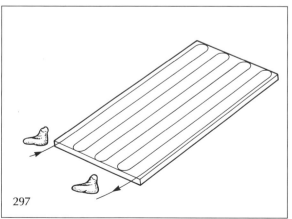

297

this should be given time to take place (*see* page 47). Another factor is the type of wood being polished. Some types have more open grain than others and will require bodying-up for longer than those with close grain. If open grain is intended, the number of times each stage is repeated can be reduced with a close-grain type.

Step 4c
Cut back the surface lightly with flour paper to remove any ring marks from the previous stages. Dust off.

(296) Charge the rubber with equal quantities of polish and spirit. Use a bottle and shake well as these should be mixed first and not added to the rubber separately.

(297) Change the path of the rubber to follow the grain, bringing it round in a loop at the end of each stroke. Look carefully at the surface. Any rings of polish should have disappeared, but repeat this stage if they have not. Bodying-up is now complete.

Step 5: Finishing

The work should be left to harden for twelve hours or so before this stage begins. The purpose of finishing is to give the surface its final brightness and shine. To achieve this, all traces of oil have to be removed. If you have not used oil, then there is none to remove, but you should also carry out this stage to remove the last of the rubber marks from bodying-up and concentrate your mind on producing the final surface. There are three main methods: stiffing, spiriting off and the acid finish. The latter involves sulphuric acid and is best avoided. Burnishing cream can also be used, however, and can be substituted for stiffing and spiriting off.

Stiffing

For this, you will need a new rubber. No oil is used in this process and it is, therefore, best to begin with a completely new rubber which has not the slightest trace of oil on it. Use old, worn flour paper on the surface

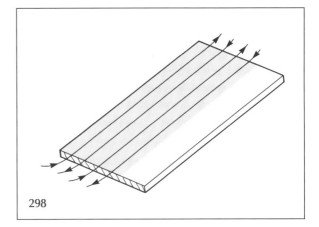

298

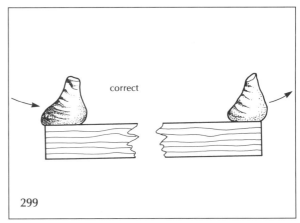

correct

299

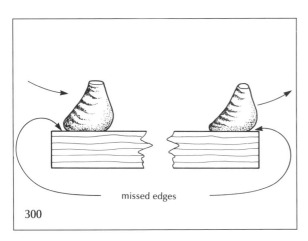

missed edges

300

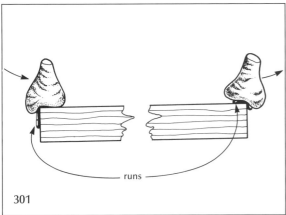

runs

301

first, very lightly. Charge the rubber with half-strength polish. Do this carefully because you need sufficient polish to flow freely but not enough to cause runs. Add the polish a little at a time, pressing the rubber on the palm of your hand to ensure an even distribution throughout. It is vital that there are no wrinkles on the face of the rubber.

(298) Glide the rubber on to the surface and off at the other end of the stroke, working along the grain and overlapping each stroke a little. Work from top to bottom, and when you reach the bottom go back to the top and repeat the process.

(299) The use of the rubber takes a little practice because it is essential to glide it on to the work at the right place. Too far in and the edges will be missed **(300)**, too soon and the rubber will not have a smooth landing and runs will result at the edges **(301)**.

Recharge the rubber as necessary, but use it fairly dry and work from top to bottom again. On each successive pass over the work, it should appear brighter as the oil on the surface is removed. The rubber should feel as though it has a little more pull and is 'stiff', hence the name given to the process. Once the stiffness is felt, it is a sign that all the oil has been taken off and the work is finished. Close inspection of the surface will reveal a few rubber marks **(302)** but these will fade as the work hardens **(303)**.

Spiriting Off

The very brightest and flattest of finishes can only be obtained by spiriting off because only the vapours of methylated spirit are used and it is a burnishing action.

Rather than treating stiffing and spiriting off as two separate finishing methods, I prefer to combine the two, stiffing first.

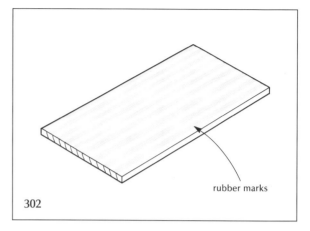

rubber marks

302

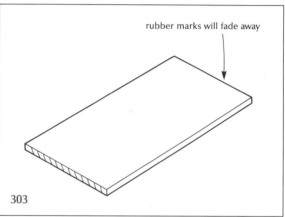

rubber marks will fade away

303

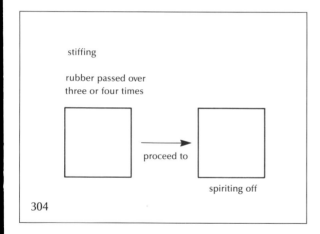

304

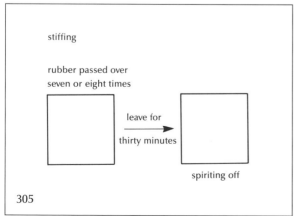

305

For the samplers, try stiffing only on a couple of them, and on a couple of others follow stiffing with spiriting off as a comparison. Every polisher has a slightly different approach.

(304)(305) Spiriting off can be done immediately after stiffing because you need the polish to be slightly soft, but not too much so. If you have not passed over the surface many times in stiffing, you can proceed straight away. If you have produced a soft surface, leave it for half an hour before spiriting. On a piece of furniture you will find that it is best to do the stiffing, leave it for an hour or so and then assess the finish before deciding to spirit off or not. Much will depend on the work in hand.

French polishing is about making judgements and deciding on a course of action. It is a demanding finish.

If the work has been left for an hour or so, it is best to go over the surface with the stiffing rubber a couple of times to soften the polish just slightly. Use a fairly dry rubber for this. Always use a new rubber for the spiriting because the process uses only methylated spirit, and no polish or oil. If you can substitute a piece of linen instead of the cotton for the rubber, then so much the better.

(306) Pour just a few drops of spirit on to the face of the wadding (a) and push it into the palm of your other hand to disperse the liquid. Cover the wadding with either linen or cotton **(307)**. It is better to have the rubber too dry than too wet because you need the vapours from the spirit on the face of the rubber and not the liquid itself. The vapours will slightly soften the top film of polish and the rubber will flatten it.

Work again from top to bottom, using circles first **(308)**, and then straight strokes with the grain and loops at the end **(309)**. Use only light pressure at first in case the rubber is too wet. Once you have established that there is no liquid being transferred to the surface, increase the pressure to quite a hard burnishing action. A good test for the correct amount of spirit is to hold the rubber to your lips – it should feel cold but not wet.

Burnishing Cream
This is another way of obtaining a mirror finish on work that has been french polished. It can be substituted for the stiffing and spiriting stages of polishing, removing any last remaining rubber marks, and can also be used as a reviver for old, polished surfaces. It is a very fine abrasive in the form of a paste or liquid and should be applied in accordance with the manufacturer's

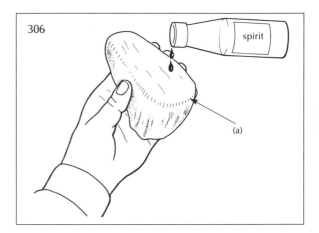

306

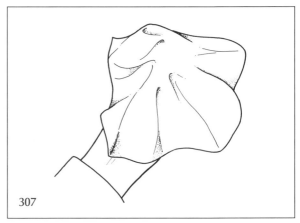

307

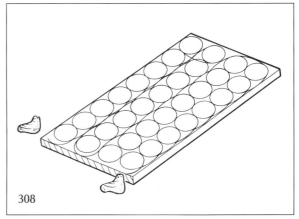

308

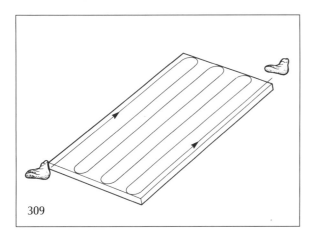

309

instructions. Normally this will require working a small area at a time with the burnishing medium on a small piece of wadding. Each area is worked over 25–30 times and is then immediately wiped dry with a soft cloth or duster.

French Polishing For a Lustre

(310) As stated earlier, french polishing is a versatile finish and does not have to be a mirror finish. A beautifully smooth, tactile surface can be obtained by polishing first and then cutting back with mild abrasives to take away the brightness. It is a good way to practise polishing because the dulling process will remove any minor imperfections in your polishing and still give a really good surface. You can stop at any stage or you can continue to a full grain finish, ending with the stiffing stage. There is no point in spiriting off, although you can if you want to gain experience.

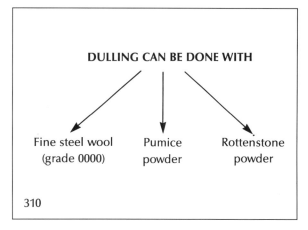

DULLING CAN BE DONE WITH

Fine steel wool (grade 0000)　　Pumice powder　　Rottenstone powder

310

(311) The only limitation to this process is the one mentioned in the colouring section (*see* page 89). If colour has been used, put a sufficient body of polish on top of it to prevent the colour being removed. Cutting back takes place in the top layer of polish only (a). If the colouring is reached, the result will be very patchy.

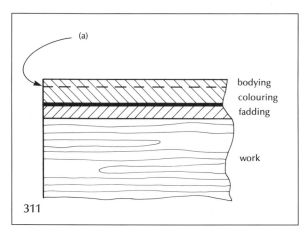

(a)

bodying
colouring
fadding

work

311

Cutting Back Method

It is important for the polish to be hard. Leave it for several days before starting the process. Cutting back can be done with very fine steel wool (0000 grade), pumice powder or rottenstone. Each will give a slightly different lustre.

(312) If you use steel wool, lubricate it with wax. Take up a little paste wax and rub with even pressure along the grain. Keep turning the steel wool to maintain the cutting action. Take care not to miss ends (a) and edges (b). Buff the surface with a soft, clean rag.

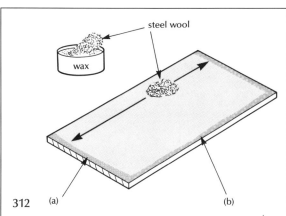

steel wool

wax

312　(a)　　　　　　　　　　　　(b)

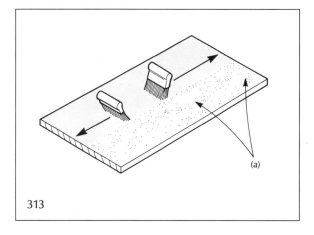

(a)

313

(313) Pumice powder (a) can be used, dry or with water. It is available in two grades (3/0 and 6/0), 6/0 being the finer. To use dry, sprinkle a little on the surface. Use a soft-bristled brush, working along the grain. Keep the strokes straight. Move the powder backwards and forwards covering the surface for an even dullness.

(314) To use pumice powder wet, sprinkle it sparingly on the surface and pour on a little water. Use a wad of soft rag arranged to give a comfortable shape to hold. It should have a fairly wide, flat base. Dip it into the water and pick up a little of the powder. Work the paste formed along the grain, evenly over the surface. Pay attention to the edges and the ends. Wash off the residue with water and a clean, soft rag which you should keep well rinsed out. Leave to dry and wipe off any remaining powder with a soft, dry cloth and check the surface for evenness of dulling. Go back to any areas that are too shiny compared to the rest. Rottenstone is the finest of the powders and it is best used wet in the same way as for pumice. Wax the surface afterwards. If the powder dries white in open grain, then use a suitably coloured wax polish, but this is not normally a problem and occurs only on the darkest of finishes.

Take great care not to cut back too far when using these abrasives. It is best to work a sampler first.

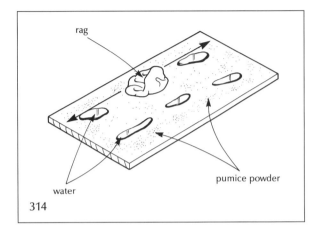

314

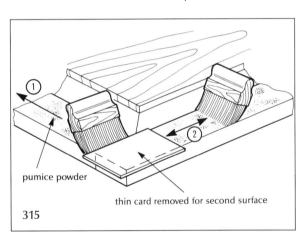

315

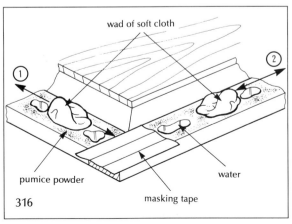

316

No matter which method is used for dulling, it is sometimes difficult to keep with the grain all of the time, such as on the corners of doors. For the dry method, you can use a piece of thin card to cover up the other surface **(315)**. For the wet method, you can apply masking tape **(316)**, but if this is used the polish should be allowed to harden well first. Apply the tape lightly and remove it as soon as possible, never use sticky tape as this tends to pull off the polish when it is removed. In both cases, without protection the surface will be scratched **(317)**.

All finishing on the panels of doors should be done before the frame is glued, as described earlier. This should include the dulling process if it is to be used on the rest of the work. The only way to see what finish each of the above will give is to try them on samplers first.

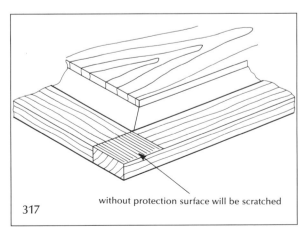

317

Dealing With Inlaid Work

Careful thought should be given to inlays at the design stage and in choosing materials for the job. Try to select a wood for the groundwork which, when given a clear finish, will result in the work being of the correct colour. In this way, the finishing will be much easier. For french polishing, keep the lighter wood on the inlays bright by using either white or transparent polish in the normal way. Use either of these to seal the surface if you are semi-waxing. Waxing or semi-waxing will require a light wax while clear varnishes and oil are used as normal.

(318) The problem arises when the colour of the groundwork (a) is too light and has to be stained. In this case, the inlays (b) have to be sealed to prevent them being stained in with the rest of the work. This is done with white or transparent polish, or you could use a shellac sanding sealer. It is intricate work and has to be done carefully for best results.

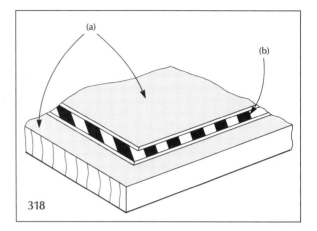

318

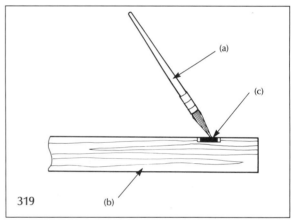

319

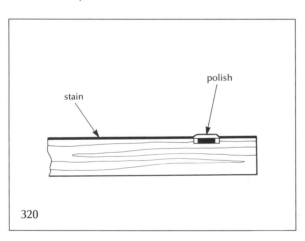

320

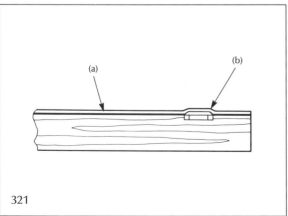

321

(319) Apply the sealer with a No. 2 or No. 3 artists' pencil brush (a). Take care not to go over the edge on to the groundwork (b) as this will leave a lighter patch when the stain is applied. If it does happen, scrape off the offending area of sealer very carefully until bare wood is reached. Two coats are needed to give full protection to the inlay (c) underneath. Use fairly thick polish.

(320) Having sealed the inlay, you can stain the rest of the work. Water stains pose no problems; spirit stains can be used but remember that their base is the same as that of the sealer. Avoid softening the seal, and remember that speed is important.

(321) Oil stains pose a problem only if you are waxing or varnishing on top. They must be fixed first by applying at least two coats of white or transparent polish with a mop (a) before continuing with the chosen finish. If a ridge is formed (b) cut it back with flour paper.

Matt and Semi-Matt Polishes

These are available for use as an alternative to cutting back with abrasives as described earlier. They are a blend of shellac, oils and nitro-cellulose. A reducer is mixed with them in varying proportions to produce a range of sheens.

Brush and Spray Polishes

Although many polishes can be brushed or sprayed, some are available which have been specially formulated for these purposes.

Advice on Use

It is generally considered that most 'special' polishes are more difficult to use than the basic ones. Some of them

---

GENERAL ADVICE ON FRENCH POLISHING

- Use only the best quality materials for rubbers
- Use raw linseed or white mineral oil for lubrication
- Do not use steel wool for rubbing down between stages
- Pay attention to working conditions – light, temperature, dust
- If stored elsewhere, polish should be at room temperature before use
- Store rubbers in glass jars
- Store polish in jars or plastic containers
- Tins should never be used for storing rubbers or polish
- Wear gloves, wherever possible, especially for modified polishes
- Always check your method on samplers first
- All shellac-based finishes require ten to fifteen days before reaching full hardness
- Do not place objects on new polish – they will leave marks
- Do not cover new work – it will cause 'blanket' marks

322

---

will require different methods of working, while others will require special thinners. Before using them, gain experience with the basic ones. Special polishes are not normally available in small quantities, 5 litres (9 pints) being the usual amount. Always use 'special' polishes in accordance with the manufacturer's instructions.

Other Polishes

In addition to the five basic polishes already described, there are many others. Red polish is used to darken light-coloured mahogany. It is normally too red and should be darkened with either black polish or spirit-soluble analine dye powders. Black polish is used in ebonizing. Both polishes can be made by adding dye powders to button, garnet or French polish.

High-Bodied and Fortified Polishes

These are particularly suitable for brushing. They contain a higher percentage of solids than normal polishes. They are ideal for the backs and insides of cabinets, and can also be used in normal fadding and bodying to build a substantial layer of polish on which the rest of the polishing operation can take place.

Chemically Modified Polishes

These are shellac based, and have been modified to give a slight improvement in hardness and water resistance. Use in accordance with the manufacturer's instructions as some will require a fad or two of ordinary polish first to overcome adhesion problems. With others, it is recommended that the same polish be used throughout.

Outside Polishes

These are also chemically modified to improve their exterior durability over unmodified polishes. Exterior life is restricted to a little over six months and does not compare with other exterior finishes. They provide a very hard surface for inside work.

Extra-Gloss Polishes

Known as 'Anglo-Yankee polishes', these can be used in exactly the same way as normal polishes, but they have been modified to give a higher gloss. They should be used with oil.

This is the process for making various woods black to resemble real ebony. It will work well only if a suitable wood is used as a groundwork. Ebony has a very close grain structure and to be as near as possible, it is best if the substitute wood has a similar grain. Mahogany will work well, but select your piece carefully as its grain is extremely variable. Ebonizing can also be done to good effect on open-grained woods such as oak and ash (although they will not look like ebony), the grain being left open to reveal the texture.

Finishing Method

Step 1

Fill and stain the wood. Filling the grain is essential if the wood is to resemble ebony, and can be done using black filler or with the polish. Use a black stain – either water, oil or spirit.

Step 2

(323)(324) Polishing is done with black polish. This can be purchased as such or you can make your own in a similar way as for colouring (*see* page 88) using black spirit-soluble analine dye powder added to the polish. You can use any of the polishes.

(325) Polishing is done in the normal way – fadding, bodying-up, stiffing and spiriting. Spiriting is optional since ebony is usually given a satin finish.

Step 3

(326) The polish is dulled as described earlier (*see* pages 97–8). You can use steel wool and wax, pumice

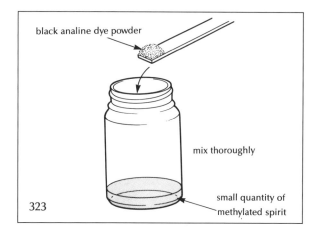

black analine dye powder

mix thoroughly

small quantity of methylated spirit

323

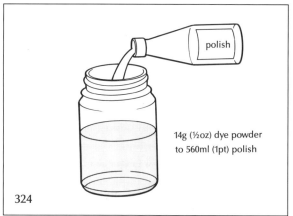

polish

14g (½oz) dye powder to 560ml (1pt) polish

324

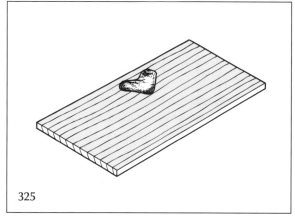

325

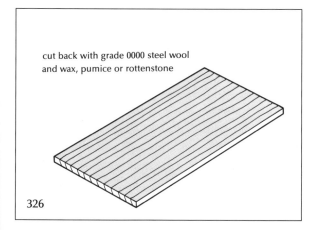

cut back with grade 0000 steel wool and wax, pumice or rottenstone

326

powder or rottenstone to give a range of lustres. Make sure there is sufficient body of polish to avoid cutting right through. Take care with the edges. Open grain is best cut back with steel wool and black wax polish to avoid whiteness being left in the grain.

(327) You can bleach a whole piece of furniture, both new and old, or it can be used to lighten a particular piece of wood in a table top, for example. If you intend to stain the work in this particular example darker, then the correction could be made with a stain, or in the colouring stage if it is to be french polished. If you want to keep the natural colour, however, the darker board will have to be made lighter by bleaching. The same would apply to a rail or leg. Ideally, you should have matched the wood right at the start to avoid the problem, but this is not always possible.

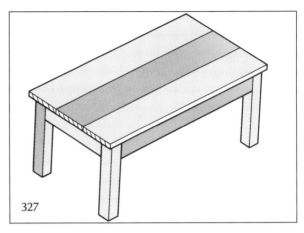

327

(328) Not all woods will bleach and some will bleach better than others. The wood is not bleached throughout, and the lightening only affects the fibres on the surface (a). All surface preparation must be done before starting the process to avoid cutting back into unbleached wood.

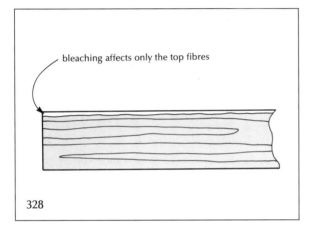

bleaching affects only the top fibres

328

(329) A number of woods that will not bleach satisfactorily are listed. Bleaching inevitably involves wetting the surface, and this will raise the grain. To keep rubbing down to a minimum afterwards, it is best to do this in the final stages of preparation. On new work, both grain raising and bleaching are best done on inside surfaces before gluing up. Outside surfaces and edges must be bleached after gluing and subsequent cleaning up.

WOODS THAT WILL NOT BLEACH SATISFACTORILY

Teak	Ebony
Rosewood	Iroko
Walnut	Satinwood
Bubinga	Padauk

You will need to test other species

329

(330) It is important to test the results on pieces of spare wood first. Bleach one half (a) and leave the other half for comparison (b). Any wetting of the surface on bare wood will have a darkening effect. The results of bleaching can only be seen after it has dried out.

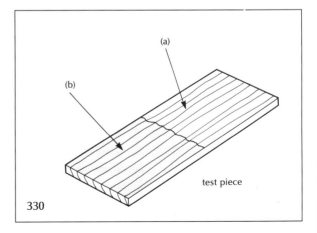

test piece

330

Always mix bleach in non-metallic containers and use special brushes which are made of grass or nylon. Alternatively, use a white cotton rag for application. Always wear gloves when handling these materials, and it is also advisable that you protect your eyes and work in a well-ventilated area.

(331) Shows the relative strengths of three bleaches.

Household Bleach

Use this if only a slight lightening effect is required. Mix one part bleach to four parts water to begin with and test the effect. Strengthen the mix if needed. Wash off the surface with water afterwards.

Oxalic Acid

This bleach is a poison and should be treated with great care. You will need to make up a concentrated solution by mixing it with hot water. Pour sufficient water for the work in hand into a jar and add the crystals until no more will dissolve. Apply the solution liberally to the surface and allow to dry. Neutralize the acid afterwards by washing it off with water and borax – use about a teaspoon of borax to 0.5l (1pt) of water.

Commercial Wood Bleach

(332) These are the best bleaches to use, and are supplied in two parts. The first part is either caustic potash or ammonia, and the second is hydrogen peroxide. It is much stronger than you will be able to buy at a chemist shop.

Application Method

Step 1
Apply part one with a bleach brush or rag to soak the surface thoroughly. Leave for five to ten minutes.

Step 2
Apply the hydrogen peroxide using a different brush or rag. The effect should be seen after ten to fifteen minutes.

Step 3
Just before the surface dries out, apply a second coat of hydrogen peroxide and leave the wood for an hour or so.

Step 4
Wash the surface with clean water. Leave to dry.

Step 5
Cut back the roughened surface with flour paper.

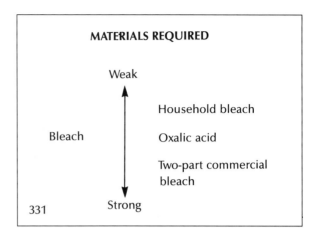

MATERIALS REQUIRED

Weak

Bleach

Household bleach

Oxalic acid

Two-part commercial bleach

331   Strong

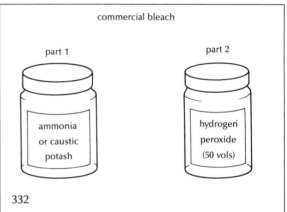

commercial bleach

part 1 — ammonia or caustic potash

part 2 — hydrogen peroxide (50 vols)

332

GENERAL ADVICE ON BLEACHING

- Do not mix together and store in a sealed container as pressure of oxygen will burst it
- Once opened, hydrogen peroxide will deteriorate and lose its strength. Stored in a cool dark place, it will keep for up to three months but it is better to use fresh bleach
- Not all woods will bleach satisfactorily (*see* Box 329)
- Test the bleach on a spare piece of wood
- Mix bleach in non-metallic containers and use grass or nylon brushes
- Wear gloves and goggles
- Work in a well-ventilated area
- Work on bare wood – remove all previous finishes using a cabinet scraper or a chemical stripper

333

LIMING – LIST OF REQUIREMENTS

1. Stain (optional)
2. Filler
3. Wire brush (if required)
4. White spirit
5. Coarse rag
6. 120 grade glass-paper
7. Flour paper
8. Finishing materials

334

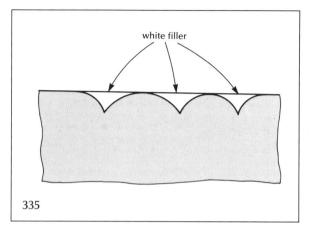

335

Liming originally consisted quite simply of filling the grain with lime and leaving white flecks on the surface. It first became popular in the 1930s and is still widely used as a finish for oak in kitchens and in picture frames. It can be used on any wood with coarse, open grain and in any situation. Although it normally used to be done on bare wood, you can use the process on top of any colour by staining the wood first. These stains can be of normal wood colours or very bright base colours such as red, green or blue. The effect this gives is ideal for more modern bedroom designs, particularly those of children, where cabin beds and brightly coloured fitted furniture are now very popular. Oak- or ash-faced manufactured boarding is widely used for this work and will take a good limed finish.

The traditional materials were oak and quicklime. Oak was used because it has an open grain and is acidic, and quicklime was used because when mixed with water it makes an alkaline solution. The reaction with the quicklime (calcium oxide) and the water also caused the latter to change into slaked lime (calcium hydroxide), which when dry is a fine, white powder. When the water and lime mix is worked on to the surface and allowed to dry, the alkaline water makes the work turn grey and the lime powder is left in the grain. This method is now obsolete as safer ways of achieving the same result are available. Unfortunately, none of these methods produce the greying effect on oak, but a similar effect can be achieved by bleaching with the two-part commercial wood bleach described in the last section. To achieve this finish the wood has to have an open grain. Good results can be obtained by using ash, chestnut or any similar open-grained hardwoods. The openness of grain can be increased by using a wire brush, brushing with the grain.

METHOD OF APPLICATION FOR UNDERCOAT PAINT, POLYFILLA OR PLASTER OF PARIS

1. Stain (optional)
2. Fix stain with two coats of Shellac sanding sealer, white or transparent french polish
3. Leave to dry
4. De-nib with flour paper
5. Apply filler
6. Cut back surplus with 120 grade glass-paper and flour paper
7. Apply finish

Note: For liming paste follow manufacturer's instructions.

336

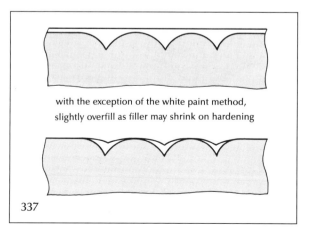

with the exception of the white paint method, slightly overfill as filler may shrink on hardening

337

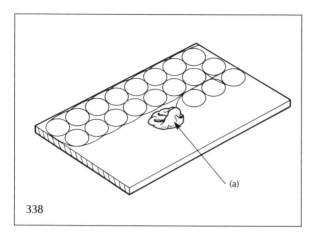

338

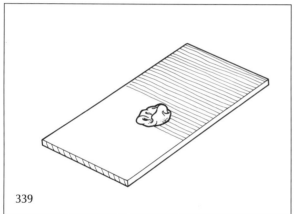

339

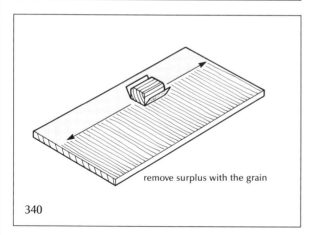

remove surplus with the grain

340

(341) A range of clear finishes can be applied on top, but a matt, satin or dull lustre will look best.

Alternatives to Lime

Liming Paste

Some liming pastes are based on water and others on oil. There are also some faster drying ones for use under lacquer. Ensure that the paste you intend to use is compatible with the finishing material – for example, oil-based paste cannot be used under lacquer. Water-based paste is a safe bet for all finishes. Some manufacturers recommend the application of a sealing coat on bare wood first to improve adhesion. If you are using stain, it is best to fix it with a couple of coats of shellac sanding sealer, or white or transparent polish after the stain has dried and before applying the liming paste. This must be done if you use an oil stain or wood dye under an oil-based paste.

White Undercoat Paint

The thicker this is, the better. As the paint is oil based, oil stain must be fixed first as with the oil-based liming paste.

Polyfilla

Available in small quantities and easy to use. Plaster of Paris could be used instead, but it sets more quickly. Both should be mixed with water to make a thick, creamy consistency.

Application Method

(338)(339)(340) These alternatives are applied in the same way as for filling the grain (*see* page 48) using a piece of hessian or denim (a).

SUGGESTED FINISHES

1. Oil-based liming paste
2. White undercoat paint
3. Water-based liming paste
4. Polyfilla or plaster of Paris

Clear satin coat varnish
Danish oil or similar
White or transparent French polish
Lacquers (do not use under 1. and 2. above)

341

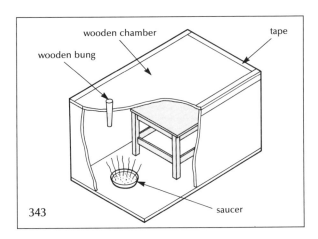

343

Fuming consists of exposing oak, which contains tannin, to ammonia fumes. As a finish, it is not widely used but it is ideal for someone with a small workshop as the requirements are minimal. It is an alternative to staining, and offers a range of tones from just slightly darker than the natural oak to almost black.

The amount of tannin in the wood and the time it is exposed to the ammonia fumes bear a distinct relationship to the final colour. The pieces of wood that have less tannin must be exposed for a longer time than those containing more tannin in order to arrive at the same colour. It is best to use the same species of oak, and preferably pieces from the same tree, to obtain the most even colouring. A piece made from bits of wood from various sources is unlikely to produce a good result.

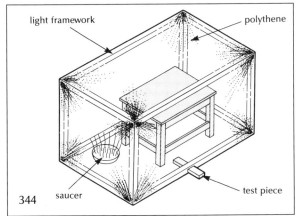

344

It is just as important with this finish as with any other to make sure that all traces of glue are removed. Try to avoid transferring grease from your hands, as well, since both will prevent the fumes reaching the surface of the wood and will cause light patches. The main requirement of the finish is an airtight container. This can be made of wood (343) but clear polythene stretched over a wooden frame (344) is better as you can see when the correct colour has been reached. Secure the polythene to the frame with drawing pins or staples (345).

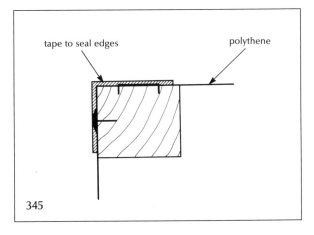

345

If you are using a wooden chamber, drill a hole in one side and prepare a wooden bung from the same material as that being fumed. It should be a tight fit and extend into the chamber. You can remove this at regular intervals to check progress. Whether viewed through polythene or by looking at the wooden bung, remember that the colour will darken still further when you apply the finish. A dab of water will give an indication of a clear finish, but an oiled finish will give a warmer tone, so test with a spot of oil instead of water. You will find some colour change takes place after only a few minutes. Frequent checks are essential.

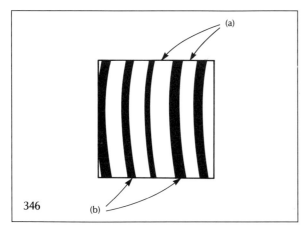

346

This finish is best done on woods that have distinct annual rings, and can be used on softwoods and hardwoods. Ordinary pine (deal) and hemlock respond to this treatment very well and are easily obtained locally. Hardwoods such as oak, ash, elm and chestnut also all burn well. The technique is very effective when used on furniture in a rustic-style setting and for exposed beams where the use of dark varnish stains can look 'plastic'. The most appealing part of this finish is that all cleaning up is eliminated except for the removal of glue and knife lines. Preparation can be left with the smoothing plane whether there are tears or not.

(346) If you look at the end of a piece of pine, you will see that one light and one dark ring is formed each year. The light wood (a) is made in the spring and summer when the tree is growing at its fastest, and this ring is soft. The dark rings (b) are formed in the autumn and winter when growth is limited, and these are harder.

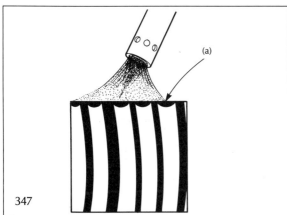

347

(347) When scorched with a blowlamp, the softer wood burns deeper (a) than the harder wood.

(348) When the grain is brushed with a wire brush, it takes on a ribbed effect, as the softer wood brushes deeper.

(349) Knots burn only minimally and are, therefore, left slightly proud of the surrounding wood (a), adding to the overall effect. Because they also contain more resin, the blackening effect is less and they can either be left a lighter colour or given an extra burn with the blowlamp to make them the same colour as the rest of the work.

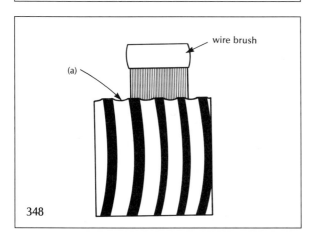

348

It would be wrong to give the impression that the finish must be black. It is true that the hard grain lines stay black after brushing, but the colour of the softer grain lines can be adjusted to give a progressively lighter colour, depending on how much brushing is done.

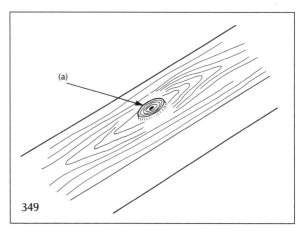

349

**BURNT AND BRUSHED FINISH –
LIST OF REQUIREMENTS**

Blowlamp or butane gas torch

Wire brush

Matt or satin coat varnish

Steel wool

Wax

} optional

350

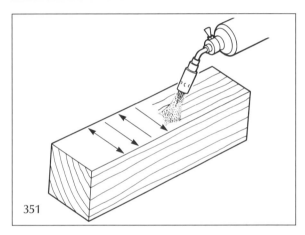

351

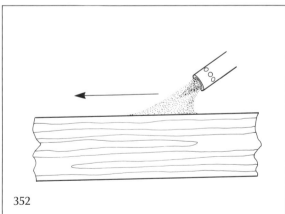

352

Do not attempt the wire brushing indoors as the carbon will cover everything with a fine, black powder. It is best done outside, either wearing a dust mask or working upwind. If you use a blowtorch in the workshop, beware of flammable materials and wood shavings.

Finishing Method

This is obviously a drastic finish and, once started, it cannot be reversed. Try the effect on a spare piece of wood first. If you use a 75mm (3in) square of pine or hemlock for the test, you will have two ends and four sides on which to see the different effects that are obtained by brushing lightly or more thoroughly. The wood always darkens when the varnish is applied because the brush picks up some of the carbon, no matter how carefully you dust off the surface.

Step 1

(351) You need a fierce flame to scorch the surface of the wood quickly. Try to work evenly across the piece from side to side **(352)**. Slope the flame towards the next area to be worked, as this will dry off the top fibres of the wood so that they are ready to be scorched in their turn – this helps to obtain an even surface. Keep the flame moving steadily all the time. Burning the end grain takes longer so the flame should be moved more slowly.

Step 2

(353) Use a wire brush to brush out the grain. Hand brushing is best – cup brushes used with an electric drill leave circular scratches even if used on their edge and it is difficult to obtain an even finish with wire wheels. Work the hand brush forwards only in order to keep the carbon dust (a) ahead of the brush. If you brush backwards and forwards, you will work the carbon back into the grain. The more you brush, the lighter the surface will become in between the dark grain lines – it can be made almost as light as the original wood.

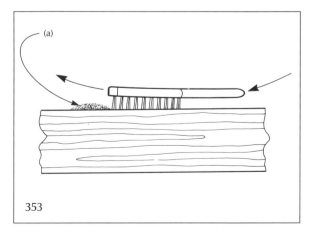

353

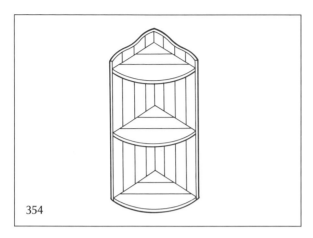

354

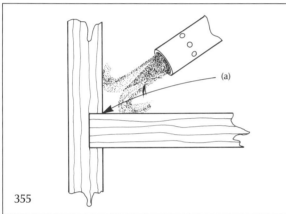

355

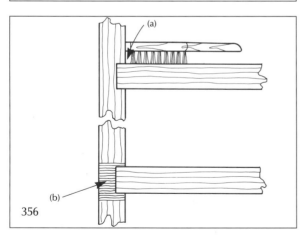

356

Step 3

A high gloss is unsuitable for this finish. Apply a coat of either matt or satin varnish and leave it to dry.

Step 4

As the surface is undulating, it cannot successfully be de-nibbed. Apply a second coat of varnish. Leave to dry.

Step 5

You have the option of applying more coats of varnish as required, but two are normally sufficient.

Use wax and 0000 grade steel wool for a lustre, and coarser grades if you want the finish to be more matt. Different tones can be produced by using different coloured waxes, but if you have the effect you want, use a neutral-colour wax.

Problems to Avoid

(354) The problems are best explained using corner shelves as an example.

(355) Burning and brushing should be done before gluing up. This is because it is impossible to make the flame burn an internal corner (a).

(356) It is also difficult to wire brush into a corner or where two pieces of wood meet at right angles to one another (a). The wire brush can also cause scratches (b).

After burning, apply a sealing coat of varnish. This enables you to clean off surplus glue without the water spreading the carbon and making the corner jet-black.

(357) Heat causes rapid moisture loss from the wood surface. Edge-jointing and levelling should be done before burning. The boards should be arranged alternately (a) or serious warping will result (b). Ideally boards should be quarter-sawn (c).

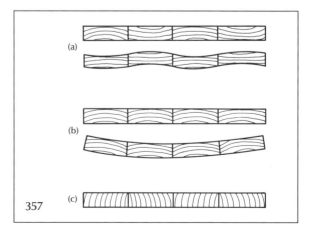

357

It is not sufficient to use edge joints that are only butted and glued. The forces set up by rapid drying can cause the joints to part. Tongue and groove joints will help, but a better edge joint is achieved by slot-screwing.

Step 1

(358) To make a slot-screwed edge joint, first mark the centres with pencil lines across the two edges to be joined, with the boards held in the vice. If there were four boards, all four would be placed in the vice.

Step 2

(359) Set a marking gauge to half the board thickness. On one board, spot the centre with the gauge on the pencil lines and, on the other, mark a line with the gauge to one side of the pencil line.

Step 3

At the spot centres, drill a pilot hole to take a 25mm (1in) No. 8 screw. Put the screws in place to leave the heads proud of the surface by about 7mm (⁵⁄₁₆in).

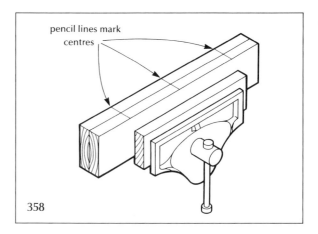

358

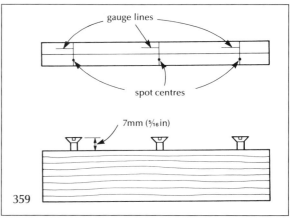

359

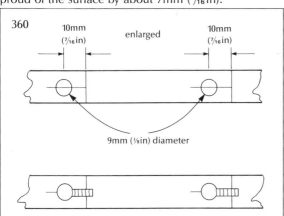

360

Step 4

(360) Drill holes which are offset by 9mm (⅜in) on the other piece. The diameter of these should be slightly greater than the diameter of the screw head – for a No. 8 screw, this will be 9mm (⅜in).

Step 5

Chisel a slot from the hole back to, and slightly beyond, the original pencil lines. This is best done with a 3mm (⅛in) chisel with the chisel edge across the grain.

Step 6

(361) Place the two pieces together and tap with a hammer until the ends of the wood are in line.

Note 1   This joint, if well done, is self-cramping and has other useful applications in cabinet making.
Note 2   Some cracking of the wood is to be expected with this finish, but in the right setting, it will only add to the overall effect.

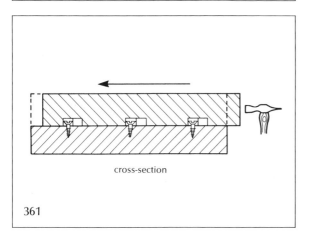

cross-section

361

Pine will darken over a period of time and become a deep orange colour. If left in bright light over many years, it will be bleached and take on a greyish tone. One method of achieving an antique appearance is to use hydrochloric acid.

You must take all necessary safety precautions when using hydrochloric acid. It will give off fumes as soon as the bottle is opened, so it is vital to work where you can avoid breathing them in. It is of little use to open a couple of windows. Instead, work outside where the fumes are taken away from you, and wear gloves and safety glasses.

(363) A variety of effects can be obtained by varying the amount of dilution and, as always, you should check on a spare piece of wood first. A good starting point is to use equal parts of acid and water. Mix them in a glass jar.

MATERIALS REQUIRED

Hydrochloric acid

Sodium bicarbonate
  or   } for neutralizing
Washing soda

Glass jar for mixing

White rag

Gloves

Safety glasses

362   *Work outside or in an extracted area*

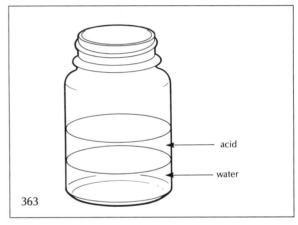

363

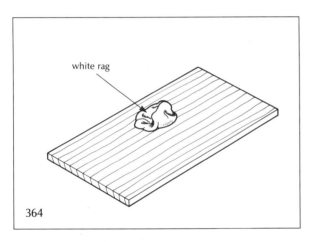

white rag

364

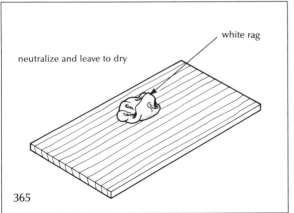

neutralize and leave to dry

white rag

365

(364) Work the solution into the surface with a white rag. You will see the effect within a few minutes. A darker result is obtained if you increase the strength of the solution up to three parts acid to one of water. A more concentrated solution will begin to give a greenish tinge; undiluted acid makes the wood bright green.

(365) Leave the acid solution on the wood for about twenty minutes, and then wash off the surface with either sodium bicarbonate or washing soda dissolved in water to neutralize it. Leave the work to dry thoroughly. As the finish involves wetting the surface, you must raise the grain in the preparation stages if you want a smooth surface as a final result. Sometimes, though, raised grain can add to the effect.

Further variations of colour can be achieved with coloured waxes. These waxes can also be used on their own to 'antique' pine. Pine can also be fumed with ammonia which will give a more yellow colour.

MATERIALS REQUIRED FOR:

REMOVAL OF OLD WAX AND DIRT
White spirit and either rag or very fine steel wool
(grade 0000)

REMOVAL OF DIRT, WAX AND TOP FILM OF
POLISH UNDERNEATH
Furniture reviver

REMOVAL OF ALL THE OLD FINISH
Small areas: cabinet scraper
Large areas, complete piece of furniture and
carvings: paint stripper

REFINISHING
Stains, french polishes, oils and waxes to suit the
work in hand

366

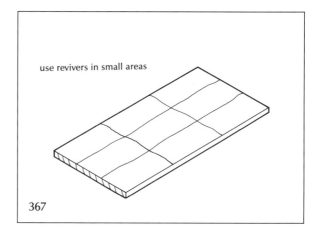

367

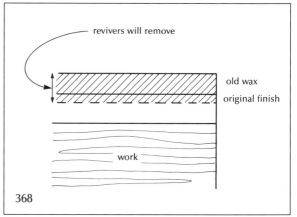

368

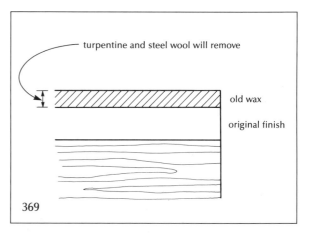

369

There is not room here to become involved with restoration work in any detail. However, I cannot leave the matter out altogether.

When faced with an old piece of furniture, the most difficult decision to make is whether to strip off the old finish and completely repolish it, or to repair it, make good the most serious damage and then carry out a limited repolish. A good clean may be all that is required. If the piece is a true antique, stripping will almost certainly reduce its value and should be avoided. Its patina – the finish built up over many years, including dents and scratches, but most importantly its colour – will be lost if stripping is carried out. In this case, restoration work must be limited to reviving the old finish. Reviving involves gently removing the old, dirty layers of wax polish which have built on top of the base finish underneath. It will leave the whole piece looking cleaner and will make any inlay work look brighter.

There are numerous revivers available, but you should exercise caution as to choice and where they are used. Some products are more powerful than others and could be described as mild strippers. It is always advisable to test a small, unseen part of the work first, before rushing in to work on the top surface of a valuable table. Most revivers contain a mild abrasive held in suspension in a solvent which will clean and burnish at the same time. They are best used on a small area at a time, working gently with the grain and then buffing up the surface with fresh wax polish afterwards. Clean off old wax using white spirit and a rag or very fine steel wool, again working with the grain.

If revivers will not do all that you require, you can opt for limited stripping. This is when you decide that for the most part the finish is good, and only a part of the piece needs to be stripped. With occasional tables or nests of tables, the frames are normally good but the tops are sometimes beyond revival.

(370) Carver chairs and armchairs are generally sound except for the tops of the arms and the top of the back where the colour of the polish (and sometimes the stain as well) has been completely worn away. In these cases, it is best to use a cabinet scraper to remove the old finish down to bare wood.

(371) Clean up the surface thoroughly with abrasive paper. restain and polish to match the rest of the work, protecting any fabrics by masking off these areas with tape (a).

(372) On larger areas or on carved work, it is best to resort to strippers and a stiff brush. There are a number available, some of which are only suitable for certain finishes. If you are unable to identify the old finish, use an all-purpose stripper which can deal with any type of finish.

Strippers can be dangerous materials to use. Always work in a well-ventilated area. Wear gloves and protect your eyes.

Strippers are normally applied liberally with an old brush. They are left for a while so that they are given a chance to lift and peel the finish from the wood underneath. The lifted material is removed with a paint scraper on flat surfaces, and a stiff brush on moulded edges and carved work.

Some strippers need to be neutralized before a new finish can be applied. Follow the manufacturer's instructions for this operation as it is extremely important.

It may seem a good ploy to take the piece of furniture to a firm which strips old doors. This is normally done by dipping the whole piece in a tank of caustic solution; the process is not to be recommended for furniture as the materials used will attack the glue in the joints and make a reglue inevitable.

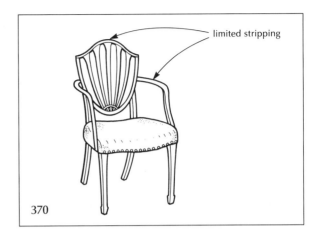

limited stripping

370

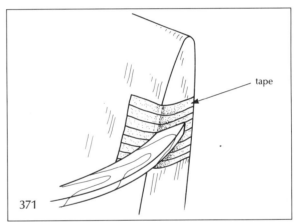

tape

371

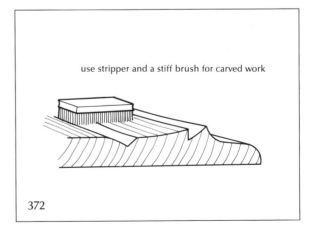

use stripper and a stiff brush for carved work

372

In some cases, particularly chairs, regluing will be an essential part of the restoration work. If so, it is better to knock the piece apart into separate component pieces and strip these individually. Cleaning up, reassembly and finishing can then follow normal procedure.

Common Faults in Old Furniture

There are a number of common faults in old furniture which can be treated in several ways.

Scratches

The treatment of these will depend on the depth of the scratch. Shallow ones which show white can be disguised by rubbing them with a Brazil or pecan nut, the oil from which will take away the white. Alternatively, proprietary scratch covers can be very effective. Deep scratches can be filled with a wax filler stick. Select a suitable colour and rub the stick across the scratch. Remove surplus wax with fine abrasive paper and a little linseed oil. Some scratches can be filled with coloured polish and a pencil brush, but some treatment with a polish rubber will be needed afterwards.

Cracks

Wide cracks can be filled with appropriate size and colour slivers of wood, glued in place. After levelling off, these are stained and the area re-finished to blend in with the whole. Small cracks can be filled with suitable fillers (see pages 43–5).

Bruises

Unless the surface is to be stripped, there is little that can be done with these. If the polish is removed, they can be lifted out with either a spot of water or a damp rag and warm iron. The steam generated will swell the grain back into place.

White Rings

These can be removed with some proprietary products which have to be rubbed in vigorously. It is really the rubbing that does the trick though, as it generates a little heat which lifts out the moisture trapped within the polish film. A mixture of half and half linseed oil and turpentine left on the surface for a while can sometimes also remove rings. Alternatively, try camphorated oil with a little judicious rubbing. Remove the oil afterwards with vinegar.

Spirit Rings

These are caused when spirits on the bottom of a glass soften the polish. Treatment of these rings will vary according to their depth. With shallow marks, it is sometimes sufficient to smooth the area with flour paper and phase in with a french polish rubber, using colour if necessary. If the marks are very deep or a groove has been cut into the polish, it may be necessary to level the area within the circle and build up with layers of polish, using a pencil brush. Coloured polish may be necessary to match up with the surrounding area. When the surface is level, use a rubber to phase in with the old polish. Use a weak polish for this last operation.

Ink Stains

Remove these with either household bleach or nitric acid. If the stain turns white, it will have to be coloured in with polish.

Finishes for Toys

The laws relating to finishes for toys that are made to sell are being changed constantly, so any stated here are likely to become out of date quickly. An example of this is that in the course of writing this book, EEC limits for heavy metals and toxins in toy products have been reduced from 300 parts per million to ninety parts per million. These stringent limits are regarded by many people in the trade to be unrealistically low, and some manufacturers will simply not bother making products which comply. The laws are obviously reviewed from time to time, and it is hoped that when this happens there will be more realistic and workable limits set.

In the meantime, those of you who wish to find the safest products should write to the various suppliers and seek assurances from them in relation to their products. More detailed information concerning the situation at a given time can be obtained either from your local Trading Standards Office or the British Toymakers' Guild. Copies of the Toy Safety Directives are obtainable from the Department of Trade and Industry.

If you make toys to sell, even on the local craft stall, it is your responsibility to ensure that the finish does comply with the limits in force at the time. If you make toys for your own children, you can use any finish you deem to be safe.

Lacquers provide an alternative to french polishing. They have the advantage of providing very good heat-, water- and alcohol-resisting properties, together with speedy and relatively easy application – although some practice is advised first. Most furniture today is finished using these materials, which are almost universally applied using various spraying methods.

(373) A look through some catalogues will reveal a bewildering array of lacquers, but they can be divided broadly into three main groups. Those offering the greatest resistance to abrasion, heat and chemicals are the two-part acid catalyst lacquers. Next are the pre-catalyst lacquers which have good resistance, but which are generally regarded as being slightly inferior to two-part lacquers. Cellulose lacquers have the least resistance, but are more resilient than french polish.

Described here are two finishes that are suitable for use by the hobbyist, where application by brush is the only system to achieve these hard-wearing surfaces.

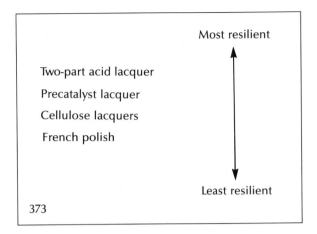

Most resilient

Two-part acid lacquer

Precatalyst lacquer

Cellulose lacquers

French polish

Least resilient

373

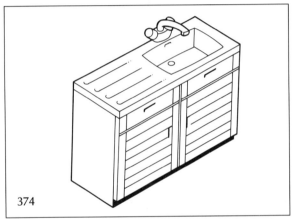

374

(374) Brushing lacquers have to be flowed on and this can cause difficulties with vertical work and that involving a lot of corners and edges, such as the underframes of tables. It is worth considering an alternative finish for these and using lacquer just on the tops. This is also true of kitchen cupboard doors and drawers, which are best removed and laid horizontally to apply the finish.

Two-Part Acid Lacquer

This is sometimes known as two-part cold-cure lacquer, or plastic coating. It is readily available in small packs which contain the lacquer, thinners and burnishing cream. Burnishing cream provides a nib-free high-gloss finish, but by using various grades of steel wool it is possible to achieve a wide range of satin lustres. By using a different method of application, you can also produce a finish very similar to oiled wood.

LACQUERING – MATERIALS REQUIRED

Grain filler (optional)

Stain (optional)

Lacquer

Hardener   } can be purchased

Thinners   } as a pack

Burnishing cream

Glass jar or polythene container

FOR MIXING

Good-quality paintbrush

Grade 600 wet-and-dry paper

Steel wool (grades 0000, 000, or 00)

FOR VARIOUS LUSTRES

Steel wool (Grade 0 or 1 for matt)

375   Clean, soft rag

High-Gloss Finishing Method

Step 1
Fill the grain and stain as required. Use only those stains recommended for a particular lacquer as the catalyst can change the colour of some of them. Stain can either be applied to the wood or mixed with the lacquer.

Step 2
(377) Mix together both lacquer and hardener thoroughly in a glass or polythene container – if a metal container is used, the acid catalyst will react with it and prevent drying. Measure it out carefully in the proportions recommended by the manufacturer and add stain if required. You can keep mixed lacquer in a refrigerator in a sealed container for several days. If left in an open container, its shelf life is reduced considerably.

Step 3
(378) Using a good quality paintbrush, apply the

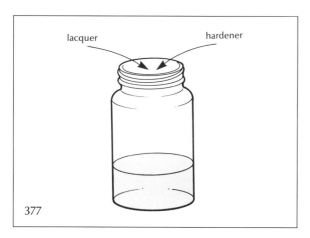

377

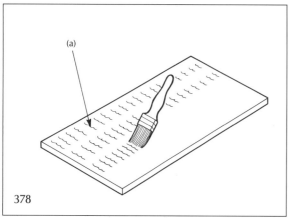

378

METHOD OF APPLICATION

FULL GRAIN AND HIGH GLOSS

Apply first coat

Leave to harden (minimum of two hours)

De-nib very lightly (grade 600 wet-and-dry paper)

Apply second coat

Leave to harden (minimum of two hours)

De-nib very lightly (grade 600 wet-and-dry paper)

Apply third coat

⌐ Leave to harden thoroughly for
   at least twenty-four hours

   Apply burnishing cream

   └──▶ Apply fourth coat if needed

376

lacquer with the grain. It must be applied liberally and, unlike paint or varnish, it should not be brushed out. You must avoid going back to the lacquer which you have already applied, even if there is an area that looks dry. Drying is quick and will cause the brush to pull after only a few minutes. Pulling will leave ripples (a) on the surface because the lacquer will be too tacky to flow easily. Dry areas are best left and corrected with the next coat. On large areas, it is important to keep a wet edge and work must proceed quickly. With regard to drying, attention must be paid to working conditions if problems are to be avoided. An ideal temperature for drying is 18°C (65°F) – the first coat will dry in about one hour, but it will not be hard. Leave it for two hours if the room is warm, and slightly longer if the room is a little cooler.

Step 4
De-nib lightly with 600 grade wet-and-dry paper used dry, and dust off.

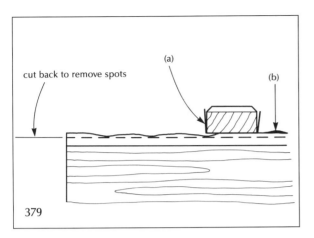

cut back to remove spots

(a)

(b)

379

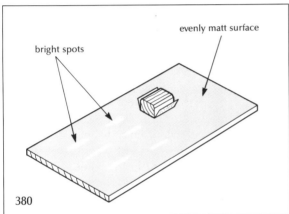

bright spots

evenly matt surface

380

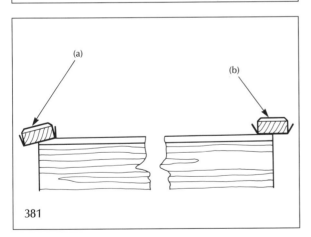

(a)

(b)

381

begins to pull a little, polish off the excess cream with a clean, soft rag, working with the grain. Assess the surface. Either move to the next area if it is sufficiently bright or do a little more rubbing with the cream. If the surface remains misty, it should be left longer to harden.

Step 5
Apply a second coat as in Step 3 and leave to harden.

Step 6
De-nib lightly with 600 grade wet-and-dry paper used dry again, and dust off.

Step 7
Apply the third coat and assess the finish; on open-grained woods without filler, a fourth coat may be necessary. After the last coat, whether it be third or fourth, leave the work for at least twenty-four hours, and preferably longer to ensure that it has hardened. This period is related to room temperature. Err on the side of caution if you are in any doubt.

Step 8
(379)   Rub down with 600 grade wet-and-dry paper. Use a glass-paper block (a) and water (b) for this operation. Work with the grain. Clean off the surface with lukewarm water and a soft cloth, working with the grain.

(380)   When dry, the lacquer should be matt all over. If there are bright spots, it is an indication that a little more work with the wet-and-dry paper is needed.

(381)   Take care not to cut back into the wood, especially at the edges. Avoid dubbing over the edges (a) by keeping the block flat (b).

Step 9
(382)   Apply the burnishing cream with a soft, clean cloth or stockinette. Work a small area at a time as shown, using hard pressure at first, and gradually reducing this as the rubbing proceeds. When the cloth

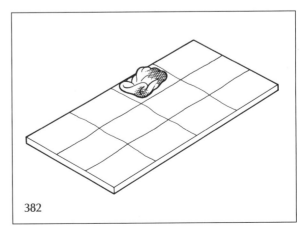

382

Satin, Lustre or Matt Finishing Method

These finishes look best with an open grain, but use then on a full grain if you wish. In this case, the lacquer is applied as before, but steel wool instead of burnishing cream is used after the last coat has hardened.

Step 1 (Optional)
Stain as required and leave it to dry; alternatively, mix the stain with the lacquer if you wish.

Step 2
(383) Prepare the lacquer by mixing it with the hardener in the correct proportions. Add a quantity of thinners which is equal in volume to the mixed lacquer.

Step 3
Apply the mixture with either a brush or a rag. If you use a brush, apply it to a small area at a time and wipe off the surplus with a rag as the work proceeds. This must be done before the tacky stage is reached. Alternatively, apply the lacquer liberally with a rag, and wipe off the surplus with a separate piece. Rags should be lint-free; old cotton shirts, pillowcases or sheets are ideal. Leave the first coat to harden for two hours.

Step 4
De-nib the surface using wet-and-dry paper or flour paper and dust off.

Step 5
Apply the second coat using the same method as the first (Step 3) and leave it to harden. You should access the surface at this stage as you have the option of applying another coat if you want to. Either apply a third coat after two hours or leave it to harden for at least twenty-four hours if you intend to apply only two coats.

Step 6
This stage puts the final finish on the surface. You have several choices and you should try each on samplers before deciding which is the most suitable.

(384) The finish is produced using steel wool (a) with a little wax polish to provide lubrication. Fine steel wools will give a higher lustre than coarse ones. Use the steel wool with the grain and leave for a few minutes before buffing with a soft cloth. On open-grain finishes, it is best to use a wax of suitable colour. Light wax on

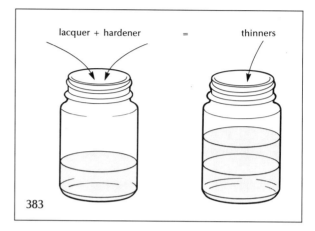

lacquer + hardener = thinners

383

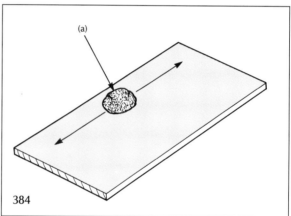

(a)

384

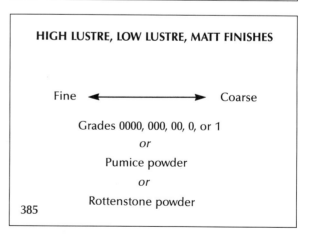

HIGH LUSTRE, LOW LUSTRE, MATT FINISHES

Fine ←————————→ Coarse

Grades 0000, 000, 00, 0, or 1

or

Pumice powder

or

Rottenstone powder

385

dark woods can dry light in the grain. You could use pumice powder or rottenstone as described in the french polishing section (*see* pages 97–8) instead of steel wool and wax. Coloured wax can be used to take the white out of the grain.

Problems to Avoid

(386) Finishes that take time to dry, and especially those that are applied thickly, pose the continual problem of dust and hairs. My advice is always to de-nib between coats for the best finish.

(387) If you do not rectify any problem between coats, foreign matter will become buried in the surface. Debris on the surface of the first coat will be impossible to remove after the application of further coats. The clarity of this finish, when used clear, is especially good, so you can imagine the problem if a dark hair is left on the surface of the first coat when the groundwork is very light – the same would apply to light specks on dark ground.

(388) You should plan the work in order to complete coatings in one day, making sure that the temperature is high enough (18°C or 65°F). Drying is by cross-

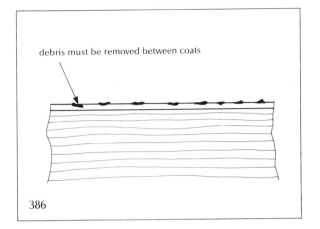

debris must be removed between coats

386

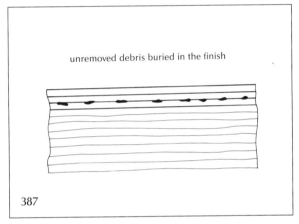

unremoved debris buried in the finish

387

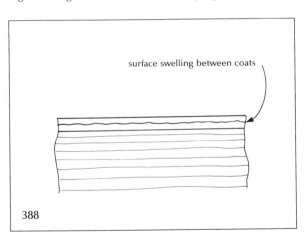

surface swelling between coats

388

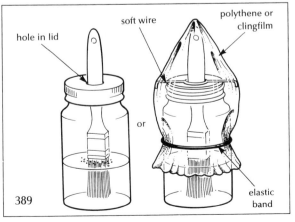

hole in lid

soft wire

polythene or clingfilm

or

elastic band

389

polymerization and not by evaporation. This reaction passes through a critical stage, and if you apply another coat at this stage it will affect the film on the surface of the one underneath – the film is soft enough to be affected by the solvents in the next coat, but is not hard enough to be dissolved again. This can cause the surface to swell and will give a wrinkled finish. If this happens, the only solution is to leave the work to harden in a warm room for several days. It is impossible to tell when the critical stage is reached as it is dependent on temperature, but it is normally between twelve and twenty-four hours. The only solution if you really are unable to complete the work in one day is to work on a sampler alongside the finished piece. Test fresh coats on the sampler first.

(389) Brushes should either be washed after each coat with thinners and detergent, or stored suspended in the lacquer as shown in the diagram.

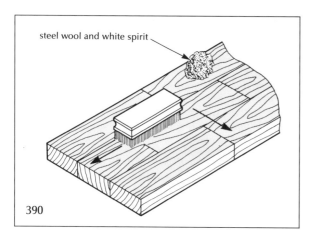

steel wool and white spirit

390

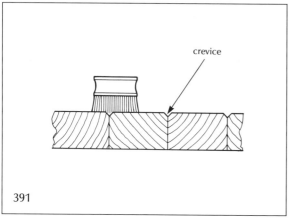

crevice

391

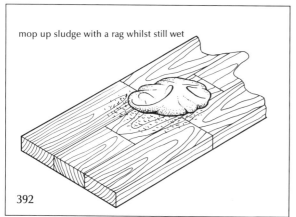

mop up sludge with a rag whilst still wet

392

Other Uses for Two-Part Acid Catalyst Lacquers

Plastic coating is available in black and white. It provides a more durable nib-free surface than paint, and the white will not turn yellow. Black can be used on solid wood or manufactured boarding to make it resemble black ash furniture. The best effect is obtained on open-grained woods. Using an appropriate stain in a range of basic colours with clear acid lacquer on top, many bright finishes can be obtained.

Old Floors

The advantage of using lacquer instead of varnish on floors is the fast drying time – two hours instead of overnight when used in the right conditions. One made especially for use on floors is available. If you are applying lacquer to old floors, remove all traces of wax, as this will affect drying.

Finishing Method

Step 1
(390) Remove the old wax using steel wool and white spirit. Every trace of wax must be removed, including that in crevices and in the grain. A nail brush worked with the grain and in the direction of joints must be used after the steel wool **(391)**.

(392) Sludge must be wiped off whilst still liquid. Replace the wiping rag regularly.

Step 2
(393) After drying scrub with detergent and water first,

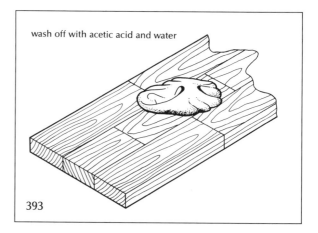

wash off with acetic acid and water

393

then wash thoroughly again using warm water to which some acetic acid (white vinegar) has been added.

Step 3
Allow at least twenty-four hours, or until the floor is completely dry. Then apply two or three coats of lacquer.

Bar-Top Lacquers

As their name suggests, these lacquers have extremely good resistance to heat, alcohol and abrasion, making them suitable for the tops of furniture which is likely to experience fairly rough treatment. They have limitations when applied to vertical surfaces because, like the two-part lacquers, they must be flowed on to the surface. Drawer fronts and cupboard doors should be laid horizontally. Bar-top lacquers require special thinners and these must be the ones recommended by the manufacturers. Anti-bloom thinners can be used where working conditions are colder and damper than would be ideal. This makes them ideally suited for on-site work in the building trade as well as for furniture. Retarders can also be mixed with them to slow down the drying time.

Finishing Method (Intended as a Guide Only)

Step 1 (Optional)
Fill and stain using those products recommended by the manufacturer.

Step 2
Apply the first coat liberally, using a good-quality brush to flow the lacquer on to the surface. Leave to harden.

Step 3
Use 600 grade wet-and-dry paper (used dry) to de-nib the surface, and dust off.

Step 4
Apply second and third coats, de-nibbing between coats. Slight thinning of the lacquer can be advantageous as it allows more time to keep a wet edge, but there are maximum recommended limits. Alternatively, a retarder can be used. A fourth coat can be applied if required. Leave to harden overnight.

Step 5
Use 600 grade wet-and-dry paper with a block, but use turpentine or a turpentine substitute as a lubricant instead of water.

Step 6
Finishing is completed using a pullover – a solvent that will soften the top film of the lacquer, knit it together and give the brightness to the finish. It does the same job as methylated spirit in the final stages of french

---

MATERIALS REQUIRED

Filler and stain (optional)
Lacquer
Thinners
Anti-bloom thinners (optional)
Retarder (optional)
Pullover solution
Good-quality brush
Glass jar or polythene container to hold liquid
Grade 600 wet-and-dry paper
Turpentine or turpentine substitute
Pullover rubber

METHOD (intended as a guide only)

Prepare surface thoroughly
Fill and stain
Stains can be added to lacquer
Smooth surface
Apply first coat
De-nib
Apply second coat
De-nib
Apply third coat
Assess finish
Apply fourth coat, if required
Leave for at least twenty-four hours
Cut back with wet-and-dry paper using
turpentine as a lubricant
Clean off and leave to dry
Use pullover solution
or
Burnish
or
Both

Weak pullover solution knits the surface together without being too severe; a medium-strength solution knits the surface together effectively with ease of application; strong solutions are normally used after spraying to remove any orange-peel effect.

394

---

polishing. Pullovers are available in different strengths, the medium ones being the easiest to use.

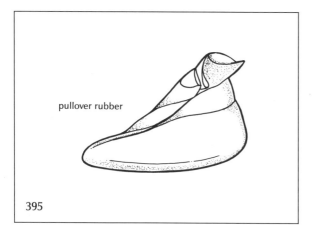

395

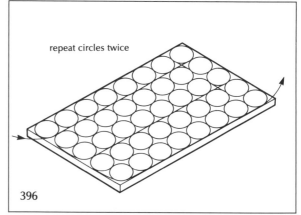

repeat circles twice

396

(395) Pullover solution is applied using a rubber. The best rubbers to use are made with wadding and thin chamois leather, but you can use wadding and cotton cloth. They are made in the same way as for french polishing. Pour a little of the pullover solution into the wadding and press on the palm of your other hand or a piece of clean wood to ensure even distribution throughout. The rubber should be moist but not wet, and its face must be free from all wrinkles. Use light pressure at first to establish the wetness of the rubber.

(396)(397) Working from top to bottom, use circles first and then figures of eight to knit the surface together.

(398) Finish with straight strokes with the grain. On small work, these will glide on and off the surface at each end; on larger work, that will not be possible. In the latter case, divide the length mentally into sections, working each in turn and taking care that you obtain the gliding action. At no time must the rubber be allowed to stop on the surface.

Step 7

Burnishing can be used as an alternative to pullover solution, or pullover can be used first to make the burnishing easier. Whichever course of action you decide to take, four days must be left before burnishing, either after the last coat has been applied or after pulling-over. This allows full shrinkage to take place and the lacquer to become sufficiently hard. Choose a burnishing cream that is specifically for use with two-part lacquers. Bar-top lacquers can also be used as a base coat for semi-waxing, as an alternative to varnish or french polish.

Note   The method described is a general one to give an

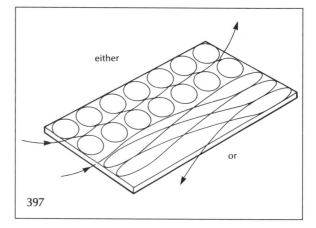

either

or

397

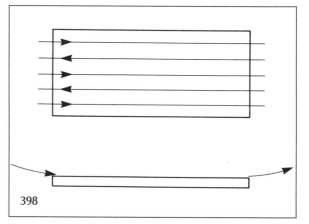

398

insight into the processes involved with these finishes and what can be achieved by using them. It is important that all instructions on a product are adhered to in respect of drying times before recoating, mixing proportions and whether or not sealers or base coats are required.

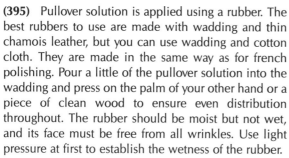

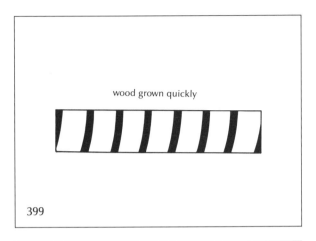

wood grown quickly

399

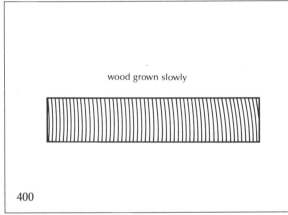

wood grown slowly

400

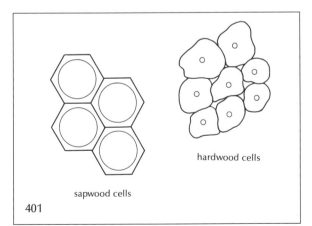

sapwood cells

hardwood cells

401

Replacing rotten exterior woodwork, whether fencing posts or window frames, is a time-consuming and expensive business. Much can be done to prevent the necessity for replacement by using hardwoods instead of softwoods, and also selecting timbers are relatively resistant to decay. Oak posts for fencing and iroko or teak for your garden seat are good choices, but the use of preservatives will help woods keep their colour and prevent fungal growth as well as making them last longer.

(399)(400)(401) If softwoods are used, careful selection of the wood and the use of preservatives prior to painting a window frame, for example, will increase its life expectancy greatly. It is best to choose wood that has grown slowly. You can recognize a good piece of softwood by looking at the colour – the darker, the better. The annual rings should be narrow and tightly packed together. This makes it more resistant to decay. It is important to reject any part of the wood that is sapwood. This will always rot quickly because the cells are open, making it very spongy and the wood will not only soak up moisture, but will retain it. Heartwood cells are more dense.

(402) When making frames that are to be painted, 'clear' preservative can be used either by dipping or brushing before the paint is applied. The best method is to place the piece with the bottom rail submerged in a shallow trough of preservative. Use a brush to wash over the rest of the frame two or three times. Leave it to soak for half an hour before draining off. You must allow sufficient time for the preservative to dry before painting, or the paint will not dry. All frames should be fitted and primed before glazing. These preservatives, based on a petroleum-distillate solvent similar to white

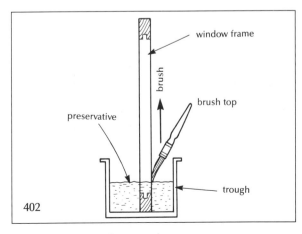

window frame

brush

brush top

preservative

trough

402

spirit, penetrate the wood well and are also available in a range of colours if painting is not required. They are also suitable for fences, garden seats, sheds and pergolas. They are not plant-friendly when being applied, but are safe when dry.

(403) Because of their high penetration, the petroleum-based products are ideal for work in contact with the ground. Large timbers should be left to soak for twenty-four hours.

Clear preservatives can be used under varnishes and polyurethanes as well, but these, like paint, will peel in time and have a high maintenance level. For work which is not in contact with the ground, there are micro-porous wood finishes that provide an alternative to paint and varnishes, both of which seal the wood completely.

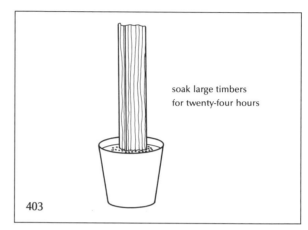

soak large timbers for twenty-four hours

403

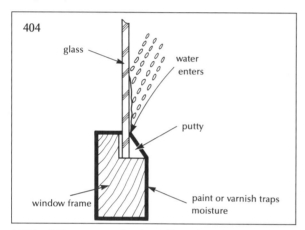

404

glass
water enters
putty
window frame
paint or varnish traps moisture

(404) Sealing the surface against moisture might seem ideal. The seal must be applied to dry wood when the finish is new. However, once water has entered the wood, the seal also prevents drying out and the moisture is trapped.

(405) Microporous finishes allow the moisture within the wood to escape as a vapour, but do not allow water to enter in droplet form. They have high-performance and low-maintenance levels as there is no peeling. They are available in either a solvent or water base. The solvent varieties are generally regarded as being harder and more durable, and are ideal for joinery. Water-based ones are more suitable for fences and sheds.

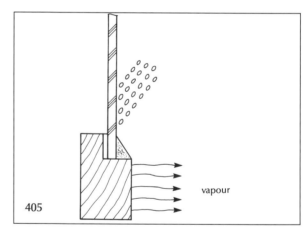

vapour

405

Finally, there are the tar-oil-based products, more commonly known as creosote. This is poisonous to plants and animals and has been largely superseded by the other products described above. A good preserva-tive, which can be used in some situations, is old engine oil. It can be used to soak the ends of posts that are to be set in concrete; soak for as long as possible.

(406) Exterior woodwork lasts longer if thought is given to the problem at the design stage. Posts do not have to be set in the ground, and timber will last a great deal longer if a good air flow is provided under sheds and summer houses. A bolt set into concrete and into a blind hole in the post allows a free flow of air.

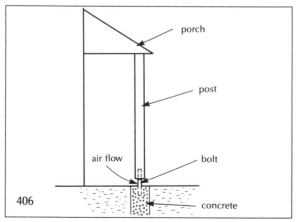

porch
post
air flow
bolt
406
concrete

Alternate grain Difficult grain present in some woods which makes cleaning up more difficult.
Aluminium oxide An abrasive used in cleaning up.
Ammonia Used in bleaching and fuming.
Analine dry powder Colour used in stains and french polish. Water- or spirit-soluble.

Beaumontage Coloured filler sticks of either wax or shellac.
Beeswax A wax obtained from the comb of the honey bee.
Bleaching The process of making the colour of bare wood lighter.
Bluing A blue mark on the surface caused by moisture and steel in contact with some woods.
Bodying-up The process of applying numerous layers of french polish with a rubber.
Burnishing Rubbing hard, normally with a cream to produce a high gloss.
Button polish A french polish with a golden colour.

Cabinet scraper Tool used to clean up and remove tears prior to using abrasives.
Carcases Constructions which have wide, flat surfaces, such as bookcases and cabinets.
Carnuba wax Wax obtained from the leaves of Brazilian palm trees.
Charging Adding polish to a french polishing rubber.
Colouring Stage used in french polishing to adjust the shade or tone of the finish.
Cross grain A difficult grain present in some woods which makes cleaning up more difficult.
Cutting back Levelling a surface between coats of a finish with an abrasive.

De-nib Removing roughness between coats of a finish using flour paper or steel wool.
Dubbing over Rounded edges caused by poor glass-papering.
Dulling Taking the gloss off a finish using mild abrasives.

Ebonizing The process of french polishing used to make other woods resemble ebony.

Faced boarding Veneered manufactured boarding.
Fad A piece of shaped wadding used in fadding.
Fadding Initial application of french polishes.
Flour paper A very fine glass-paper (240 grit).
Frames Constructions using small sections of wood to enclose a large area, for example, table frames or stools.

Fuming Process using ammonia which makes oak darker without using stains.

Garnet polish A french polish with a brown colour.
Glass-paper An abrasive used in cleaning up.
Glass-paper block Block with cork base around which glass-paper is held.
Grain filler Used to fill open grain.

Horn An extension of wood deliberately left protruding from a joint.
Hydrochloric acid Used for an antique pine finish.
Hydrogen peroxide A bleaching agent used with ammonia.

Interlocking grain Difficult grain present in some woods, making cleaning up difficult.

Lacquers A range of finishing materials giving a resilient finish.
Levelling Planing two pieces of wood flush and level.
Liming Finish, normally on oak, which leaves white in the grain.

Mop A special brush used in french polishing.

Naptha A solvent used in naptha/oil stain.

Oxalic acid A fairly mild bleach.

Polishing board Device used for holding loose pieces on the bench when applying polish.
Pullover A solution used with a rubber to give a final finish to lacquered work.
Pumice powder A mild abrasive used for cutting back or dulling.

Raised grain A rough surface caused by swelling of wood fibres.
Reviver Used for cleaning an old finish in restoration work.
Ripple Marks on the surface caused by a variety of errors.
Rottenstone A mild abrasive used in cutting back and dulling.
Rubber The basic tool used in french polishing.

Sealer A variety of products used to seal the surface before another treatment.
Sinking A finish which shrinks back into the grain of the wood.

Spiriting off   The last stage of french polishing.

Stain   Used to colour wood before a finish is applied.

Steel wool   An abrasive used for cutting back and dulling. Various grades are available.

Stiffing   The process in french polishing before final spiriting off.

Stopping   A filler used to disguise blemishes.

Stripper   Material for completely removing an old finish.

Tears   Where grain has been pulled out of the surface of the wood when planing.

Transparent polish   The lightest of all french polishes.

Varnish stain   Varnish with colour pigments added. Not suited to cabinet work.

White polish   Almost colourless french polish.